Peach Col.

PEACH COBBLER STORIES

**By
Suzanne Lafond**

Love to Barbara... because you love Clifton too!

*Suzanne Lafond
8.28.13*

Peach Cobbler Stories

Copyright 2013 by Suzanne Lafond.

ISBN: 978-0-9850084-2-0

Printed in the United States of America

All rights reserved. No portion of this book may be reproduced without the written permission of the author.

This book is a personal memoir and reflects the memories of the author. Content is subject to personal interpretation. The author holds no responsibility for any errors in content.

Photographs, press clippings, articles, artwork and illustrations are provided from the archives and personal collections of Suzanne Lafond & family.

Cover and various vintage photographic tintings and colorings by Eva Liorlen, Chicago.

Cover design, book layout, photo treatments, editing and production services provided by Thom W. King, KingAuthor Productions, P.O. Box 50214, Nashville, TN 37205.

Published by KingAuthor Productions, in association with Anthem Publishing, Batavia, NY

Author's website: suzannelafond.com

Email contact: lafondsuzanne@gmail.com

Table of Contents

Why Peach Cobbler Stories?   9
What My Catholic Faith Means to Me   10
The Beginning   19
Childhood Guidance and Independence   33
A Story From First Grade   39
Christmas Eve 1938   43
Summer Camp Memories   49
Five Beaver Pelts and Two Onyx Eyes   65
Memories of My Mother   71
My Father's Journey to the Olympics   83
Rodolphe Lafond: His Story   87
Petit Souvenir de Papa   91
How I Met Kermit   95
Where Did Granddaddy and I Live?   109
Tennis Fashions by Suzanne in 1969   113
Family Photos, Stories and Poems   120
Van Cliburn in Nashville   167
Life After Divorce   189
Julia, Paul and Me   195
The Los Angeles Olympics 1983 & 1984   221
Back in Nashville   229
Short Stories and Poems   235
Rwanda, One Man's Story   297
1997 Granny Smith's Farewell Speech   305
Dress For Success Moments   315
Athena 2003 Awards   329
More Peach Cobbler Stories   333
Pleasant and Amusing Moments   347
A Prayer as We Grow Older   351
The Cycles of Civilization   352
Biography   353
Handwriting Analysis   357

Acknowledgements

In putting together these memories and reflections, for my seven granddaughters, I have wished to answer a few questions they might have had about my life and upbringing in Canada and what followed when I married their granddaddy, Kermit Christian Stengel, Jr.

Marc Kermit and Terry Hill Stengel's daughters are: Mary Elizabeth, Morgan Elen and Sara Sudekum – all Stengels at this writing.

Christian Sudekum and Charlotte Mutarigirwa Stengel's daughters are: Zoe Ineza and Kaia Muhiza Stengel.

Eric Lafond and Claudia Knauer Stengel's daughters are: August Knauer and Marie Sudekum Stengel.

I wish especially to thank Thom King who has been an indispensable collaborator, organizer, producer and photographer par excellence on this project.

As if that were not enough, Thom has been unflappable, supportive and a very patient project coordinator, all the while listening to my Peach Cobbler Stories. On that count alone, Thom deserves a GOLD STAR!

Thank you Thom King.

Suzanne Charlotte Lafond
Nashville, TN
June, 2013

Dedication

To the memory of my parents

Léa Moquin Lafond
1899 – 1969

Léonard dit Rodolphe Lafond
1901 - 1959

Suzanne Lafond

Foreword
By Marlene Grant Pinck

Suzanne and I met at 13 years of age and we became close and dear friends and have remained so into our 80s!

We had wonderful teen years – volunteered to work for the Canadian Red Cross, double dating and enjoying each other's company.

Life progressed; marriage, children, early widowhood for me and for Suzanne a divorce. I admire Suzy's fortitude and determination, no matter what her endeavors: Julia Child, Dress for Success, teaching French - going to Wenatchee, WA to be with her when she received the title of Granny Smith, beating out 8,000 contestants! Suzy made a success of all of them.

I hope you enjoy reading Suzanne's life story – you will not be bored!

All the best in your latest endeavor, Suzy.

Love to my dearest friend,
Marlene

Suzanne at Camp le Capitaine, Lac des Français

Why Peach Cobbler Stories?

I suppose I owe you an explanation as to why these stories are called *Peach Cobbler Stories*. It goes like this: I like telling stories, let's clarify, they are not lies, no, they are made up of true anecdotes that beg retelling, my friends encourage me, poor dears!

Eric Lafond Stengel, the youngest of my three sons, puts up with my stories, most of the time, but there are many times, on the telephone or when we are together, when he doesn't have time to listen. I understand that he is very busy, really he is. To keep me from getting too far into the telling he will ask: "Mom, is this going to be one of your *Peach Cobbler Stories*?" (*PCS*). That cracks me up every time, so generally I let him go.

What My Catholic Faith Means to Me

In a word, it has meant more than I can add up at this very moment. I have never been good at thumbnail sketches.

When I made my First Communion and was confirmed into The Catholic Faith at age seven, I took that to be a lifelong commitment. It has indeed been lifelong.

You see, I was sent to a private girls' school. In Montréal (at the time) all French Private schools were run by Nuns. The first such school I attended was Villa Maria from 1st grade through 4th grade. At the end of 4th grade, I asked my parents if I could go to Sacred Heart Convent (Couvent du Sacré Coeur) and my parents indulged me. Some of my friends attended Sacred Heart and, no small matter, I really liked the uniforms! I enrolled at Sacred Heart in the 5th grade. Both were excellent schools, both run by a different order of Nuns. From there I attended l'Ecole des Beaux Arts de Montréal and Sir George Williams Business School College.

In my immediate Lafond family, no one else practiced their religion. I was convinced, at a young age in my spiritual life, that I must be the one to pray for members of my family. It was very important for me to have God's attention because I felt a great responsibility regarding those I loved, who were close to me, and were non-practicing Catholics. My brother, Pierre, was never baptized, so he wasn't a non-practicing Catholic. I prayed for him too.

That seems to have set a pattern for my life. I have been going to Mass on Sundays and Holy days, by myself, from the age of seven up to, and including this year, 2013.

I am not the best Catholic that walked the face of this earth, but like most commitments I make, I am there. In difficult times the Church has been a refuge, in happy times the Church is the perfect setting to give thanks. Always, it has been a source of spiritual nourishment and it has given me strength. My spiritual life continues to this day.

Kermit and I discussed my being a Catholic before we were married and he was perfectly fine with that and agreed that our children would be raised in the Catholic Faith. Kermit felt it was important for children to grow up going to church. A Church they could call theirs and because I was a Catholic there was no argument or doubt that our children would be raised in my Faith.

That worked quite well until first, Marc, around age 15 or 16 decided he would no longer attend church…soon the other two brothers followed. There was no forcing them ever.

Although Kermit was very willing to have our sons attend Church, he himself did not, even though through his own family he was part of the Lutheran Faith. They, however were not church-going either.

So, once again I was going to Mass on Sundays and Holy Days by myself. Prayerful meditation is good no matter where you attend church. I enjoy the comfort of having tradition play such a big role in the Catholic Faith. It is what I know, and find reassuring and comforting.

I long ago stopped walking to church to pray to St. Anthony, the finder of lost things. I had lost my mittens and looked everywhere for them. Then it occurred to me to ask St. Anthony to help me find them…it was winter and my hands were cold. Also, I thought my mother would be angry with me for having lost my mittens – they were new. The church in Notre Dame de Grace was several blocks from my house. In the afternoon, I decided to walk to church. I prayed so hard, retuned home and finally found the mittens on the radiator of the front hall of our house. They were warm as toast.

I hoped St. Anthony would give me a prayer credit for future lost things. He did answer that prayer… they weren't lost just drying from the morning playtime in the snow.

Perhaps one of the important things religions emphasize, all religions, is the virtue of Charity. First toward God, but also toward one's self and one's neighbor. It is a lifelong practice we must never give up.

These thoughts on what my Catholic Faith means to me were never intended to be a long and ponderous spiritual discussion. On the surface, I see my continuing presence in the ranks of Catholicism as personal, not necessarily open to dissection, but simply accepted as the religion that formed me.

Peach Cobbler Stories

Suzanne, a few months old (1931), photographed in a deep maroon velvet chair trimmed with wood carvings

Suzanne with Teddy Bear

Suzanne in her favorite rocker on the balcony of her first home, an apartment on Maplewood in Outremont

Pierre and Suzanne sitting on the well at Camp Le Capitaine

Suzanne with Father's dog, a Russian Wolfhound

The Beginning

My brother Pierre was born in 1930, and I was born in 1931. We are 17 months apart in age.

Our parents were living in a part of Montreal that was mostly French-speaking, it was called *Outremont* which means "On the other side of the mountain."

Montreal is one of few islands that can boast of having a mountain. The mountain is called Mount Royal, or Mont Royal, which is where the name Montreal comes from.

Outremont was where our parents lived when we were born. It was a nice apartment, overlooking Mount Royal, but not quite big enough for our growing family. Our parents decided that we should learn to speak English. To be bilingual was an asset. My parents were not fluent in English at the time, though they did speak a little. Later their English skills would improve considerably. When they first married there was no English spoken at all, except between themselves, when they didn't want "the children to understand." To me that was an added incentive to learn to speak English.

We moved to a section of Montreal where English was much more prevalent, even though this area had a French name: *Notre Dame de Grace*, referred to as NDG, Our Lady of Grace.

Our friends and neighbors were English-speaking. My brother attended a private school called Lower Canada College, which was within walking distance, and was patterned after the British school system. I went to a private French-speaking Catholic convent, a school called *Villa Maria*.

We both learned to speak English, and I think this was one of the few times that I was actually ahead of my brother in a skill. Pierre didn't take to speaking English as readily as I did, for some reason. By the time we moved to NDG, I was already bilingual. I learned to speak English, as much as a four year old can, when we lived in Outremont. Pierre took a bit longer, but he outclassed me academically before long.

It turns out that one of our childhood neighbors, one of the local kids who literally lived next door from our family, would grow up to become an internationally acclaimed celebrity. The boy we knew as Bill, pictured on the front porch with my brother, was William Shatner, star of the Star Trek television show and movies.

My brother and Bill became good friends and got into quite a bit of boyhood mischief together. They didn't attend the same schools, but being next door neighbors, they shared some activities.

I'm not sure if Pierre would like me telling this story, but we were city kids living in a big city, even if we were in the suburbs. Pierre and Bill were playing softball in the street like all kids did at times. Either Bill was pitching and Pierre was at bat, or vice-versa, and the ball hit some guy's car parked on the street, breaking the windshield. It's not funny, but after so many years later, I have to laugh. They took the ball and bat to our house, hid them away, and promptly went to see a movie at a nearby theatre. Believing the theory that it is best to be out of sight and out of mind, they disappeared into the darkened movie house, finding safety in the theatre. As far as I know, their secret crime has remained unsolved, fading into decades of protected memories. I've dutifully guarded their reputation, as any little sister would, but must admit to feeling a bit of Catholic relief in being able to confess and share this story with future generations.

There was a vacant field a few doors down that was used by all the neighborhood kids as a playground and communal gathering spot.

Even though we all came from different backgrounds, we were friends. Some came from French families. Others from English ones. There were Jewish kids and Greek kids, all adding ethnic textures and customs to our neighborhood. It was a good area in which to grow up.

One of the things we did in summer, though it is something of an odd thing to do, now that I look back on it, was baking potatoes in the vacant field. It went like this: The boys dug a hole in the ground. When that was done, we would run back to our homes and return with raw potatoes. A fire was built in the hole, potatoes tossed on the fire and covered with dirt. This was the guys' job, while the girls looked on and teased the boys. Lo and behold, soon we were feasting on the most delicious baked potatoes we'd ever had!

Maybe the act of waiting and watching is what added to the experience, or it was simply due to eating alfresco with a group of one's friends.

Then again, it was nothing more than sitting crosslegged with the neighborhood gang, in the open air, waiting for the potatoes to bake, smelling the burning wood. Such was our unusual childhood feast. We did this only once or twice each summer. It was after all, a bit of a production.

We also played softball in that same vacant lot, at least the younger kids my age did. The street was used mostly by the older kids who were not the novices we were.

I remember my dad coming home from work one day and spotting me playing in the vacant field. He saw me pitching the softball and said I ran like a gazelle with my feet moving as fast as they could. He said he was very impressed with my game, but that my pitching arm could use a little help! I pitched like a girl you see…imagine that? Well, with softball one pitches underhand, right?

We walked to school, we played in the neighborhood, and then my mother would come to the balcony and say in her French way, *Suzanne, Diner* and all the other kids would repeat the way she called me to dinner. Since it was not a French-speaking area, they mimicked her words and her voice. I didn't mind. I was always proud of being bilingual.

The French-speaking people in Montreal were usually the bilingual ones, at least to some extent. My English friends never did master the French language, so I was proud of my ability to speak two languages. I didn't mind that my mother called to me in French or that my father dressed like a Frenchman. He was very much involved with equestrian events in general, wearing riding britches and a French béret, when he wasn't wearing an impressive pith helmet. With his handlebar moustache, he cut quite a dashing figure, looking nothing like the fathers of the neighborhood children. He was my dad and I was proud of him.

We started calling our father "Pops" instead of *"Papa"* when we moved to NDG, where we were exposed to English-speaking neighbors.

My parents never spanked us when we were growing up. Instead, my father in his mischievous way, told Pierre and me when we were still quite young, that he had an electric spanking machine in the basement. Just the idea of that device being ready and waiting somewhere within the hidden confines of our home was more than enough motivation to keep us in line.

For years, I refused to go down to the basement out of fear. My brother, being 17 months older, didn't seem to be terribly threatened by the idea. I don't remember ever having a conversation with him about the impending doom machine, at the time. Much later, we talked about "La tappeuse électrique," with much laughter. Later, Pops liked to laugh about this make believe invention. Really we were good kids, so no harm was done either way. It still brings a smile to Pierre and me when we remember those times together.

Being a parent and a grandparent myself, these many years later, I marvel at how funny and clever my father was, where the mere idea of a non-existent spanking machine in the basement was enough to keep us on our toes.

La petite Suzanne in a party dress, age 4 or 5

Benoit Lafond, Suzanne's grandfather and father of Rodolphe Lafond

Papa, Rodolphe Lafond, in his twenties

*Maman dressed for shopping on
Ste. Catherine Street, downtown Montreal*

Top photo is Lea Moquin. Bottom photo is August Stengel replicating the 1899 photo of Suzanne's Mother. August's dear Jack Russell dog was named "Atlas." August was born Nov. 19, 1997 – almost 100 years separate these two events.

Childhood memories: from left: Suzanne (age 3), Pierre (age 4), Pierrette Lord, (approximately age 9), her brother Michel Lord (approximately age 4). Their parents, Henri and France Lord were very good friends with Suzanne's parents. In fact, Suzanne referred to them as "Oncle Henri and Tante France."

Family portrait of the Lafond family. From left: Pierre, father Rodolphe, mother Lea, and Suzanne. Pierre is loving the moment.

Papa and Pierre on Marcil Ave.

Maman with Pierre and Suzanne in their apartment on Marcil Ave., N.D.G.

Childhood Guidance and Independence

I think it is only fair to say that I've had a very contented life after all, even with its bumps, bruises, nicks, and disappointments.

I had parents who cared about me and my brother, about our education, instilling in me at a very young age the importance of independence.

My gosh, what a gift that is!

I was led to believe that I could do anything, and even if I didn't have the skills at the time, I could find out how to accomplish my goals. I was never really at a loss for anything. I became a very resourceful child because of that. It's not that they didn't want to help me, they did. Just by giving me the right attitude, I learned how to solve my own problems.

The other major gift they gave was when they decided to move our family to an area where my brother and I would be forced to speak English in an English speaking neighborhood.

That is a huge gift for which I continue to thank them 'til this day. I've used my knowledge of French/English, it is fair to say, almost every day of my life. It has given me job opportunities and a competitive edge that took me to places I could never have imagined otherwise. It was a sacrifice for them at the time. They were very comfortable in their old French-speaking neighborhood, but they had higher aspirations for our family, and were willing to take the necessary steps to accomplish that goal for their two children.

I will be forever grateful for their foresight and wisdom.

My brother Pierre and I were not close to each other in a warm and fuzzy way. That really wasn't the way our family was with each other. There was an abundance of love and devotion to one another, but it wasn't displayed in public with hugs and kisses all the time. It wasn't the custom of the day, either. I idolized my brother, but he would croak if he heard me saying that today. I never really told him how I felt at the time. Even though he was only 17 months older than me, he was always, in my eyes, tall and handsome, and I was just a little girl living in his shadow.

I didn't feel that I was up to his caliber in academia or even intelligence, even though I now think I was. I don't know why I felt that way. It wasn't anything my parents did or didn't do. Nor was it a feeling Pierre placed on my shoulders. It was self-imposed I do believe. I was concerned that Pierre saw me as a pretty little girl, a butterfly, nothing of substance. That's what I thought, even though he never said that. My own lack of self-confidence was at play, I suppose, when I compared myself to him.

Maybe because I felt that way it gave me motivation to achieve on my own. I was interested in so many things along the way and doors opened.

By nature I am adventuresome, resourceful and willing to try things, but I can honestly say I was never foolhardy. My course was somewhat unique in that no predictable avenue was followed. I was steadfast in my pursuits. If you aren't tested then you never really know what you can accomplish. I've done things I never studied for, or had any training in, or even apprenticed, and somehow I managed to find a modicum of success - perhaps by the seat of my pants.

My grades were good in school. I wasn't the strongest student in math, but I was very good at writing, and in all other subjects. In High school I was named to "Le Cercle Littéraire Barat" a literary group named after the founding sister of Les Dames du Sacré Coeur at the Couvent du Sacré Coeur in Montreal, where I was enrolled after Villa Maria.

I remember one of my early French-language teachers, *Madame Blanchard,* gave us a project in class, telling me that I was very good at being a detective, searching for answers, seeing things that give information. She said I had a gift, and those kind words stuck with me over the years. It is amazing how words of encouragement can have such profound influence on a young, developing mind, providing a safe and nurturing environment to grow and achieve. Her moments of praise yielded a lifetime of positive motivation in my life.

I can only hope that all children have a *Madame Blanchard* in their lives at those critical moments of development.

Pierre and Suzanne all dressed up!

Pierre and Suzanne Lafond in their Sunday best circa 1935

Four Little Kittens storybook: a dear and cherished wee book that captivated Suzanne as a very young child. She learned to read quite early and the worn book covers and its pages would attest to its place among favorites. This copy was found in an antique shop. A caption inside the front cover says "Our version of the antique Original." Suzanne can attest that the text and photos are true to the original!

A Story From First Grade

Here is a Peach Cobbler Story of my first grade. I attended Villa Maria, a private girls' school (we call them couvent/convent, in French). After a couple of weeks in school we were told that the English teacher would come in the afternoon to begin teaching English. I was really looking forward to that class. The teacher came in, introduced herself and showed us a variety of items - she would then say: La balle, the ball, le crayon, the pencil, le livre, the book. I thought this was going to be very boring. I wondered if I could, in some way, let her know that I could speak English.

That's it, I thought, I've got it. I raised my hand while seated at my desk. The nun said: "Yes, mademoiselle Suzanne, what is it?" I stood up and in my very best English I answered this way: "May I please leave the room?" She beckoned me with two fingers to come forward. I did and the nun said: "Where did you learn to speak English like that?" I responded, full of confidence: "With my friends!" To leave the room in my day meant to be excused to go to the bathroom.

From that point onward I accelerated to the third grade for the English period. There were three grades in one classroom at this small private Catholic school. The nuns even brought books in English for me to read on my own.

One afternoon, I was asked along with another classmate to attend a "Conversation" at L'Ecole Normale (the teaching college) adjoining Villa Maria. This was where young women were educated to become teachers. My classmate and I sat on stools on a stage where the young would-be teachers of the future gathered in the audience.

Each in turn we answered questions. The ones I was asked had to do with church attendance, where I liked to sit, etc. I answered that I liked to sit at the back of the church, when in truth I liked to sit in front of the church where I could see what was happening at the altar. In my mind, I thought that was more self-effacing for a young Catholic girl to say.

There were a variety of other questions which I do not recall 74 years later, but I do remember very well the very last question I was asked: "Do you know where babies come from?"

"Yes," I answered. "Ils sont tombés de la pensée du Bon Dieu." Translation: "They have fallen from God's thought."

The young women in the audience reacted with laughter and applause. I believed it was so and was happy that I had given a correct answer.

Fast forward when I was about nineteen years old. I was dating a young man, about the same age, named Derek Hannaford. That tells you right away that Derek was not French speaking. I dated mostly Anglos because those were the fellas I knew while living in NDG. I dated Derek several months. He was not the love of my life, by a long shot, but we did enjoy one another's company. One evening, his older brother (by five years) Jim Hannaford called me. I was surprised by the call and he proceeded to say the following: "Suzy, I am calling because there is something I would like you to know. You see, our Dad is afraid that you might have designs on Derek and if you do, we want you to know that Derek will be left out of his inheritance were you and he to marry. Neither Dad nor I would want Derek to marry a French Canadian girl." You can imagine my astonishment. To this I responded: "Jim, you or your dad need not worry because I have absolutely no designs on Derek

Hannaford. Our relationship has never been serious." With that I thanked him for his call and swore I would never speak to that pitiful and stupid family ever again.

A favorite photo! Suzanne's mother enrolled Pierre and Suzy at the Botanical Gardens of Montreal in a course called Les Jeunes Naturalistes – The Young Naturalists. Pierre is the tallest one, Suzanne is in the white sweater. Photo circa 1936

Christmas Eve 1938

I well remember that particular Christmas Eve in 1938. Most, but not all, Christmas Eves were celebrated at our house with a trip to church for Midnight Mass followed by a Réveillon prepared ahead of time by my mother. A Réveillon is a dinner which follows either Midnight Mass, New Year's Eve or a special occasion during the year.

I loved attending Midnight Mass with my family. I also remember hearing the crackling snow covered by a thin layer of ice beneath our boots as we walked toward the church.

Christmas Eve was memorable that year because of the following event that could have ruined everything:

Grand-père had come to spend the Christmas holiday from Saint Majorique, where he lived in the Eastern Townships, or we would say in French, les Cantons de l'est. Our grandfather was in our home as was his youngest daughter, Gertrude Lafond, our dad's youngest sister.

Because we would be staying up very late, my parents strongly suggested that I take an afternoon nap that day.

I went to my room and because the events of the day had me very excited, there was no way I could take a nap.

Instead, I decided to organize my own small altar on the nightstand. I had 2 candles – bigger than birthday cake candles, but not tall ones used on the dinner table. I had some tiny statues, one of Joseph one of Mary and a Baby Jesus in his crèche. I had nothing to hold the candles upright. If I were to make a believable altar, I had to have something to make the candles stand up. I said to myself, I have it! I'll cut two pieces of cardboard each in a circle approximately 3 inches in diameter. My plan was to light one candle at a time and let the candle drip fresh warm wax onto the pieces of cardboard, one at a time and the candle would stick, on the newly melted wax, as intended. I set out to repeat this process with the second candle and I succeeded in dripping warm wax onto the second so-called holder, when the first candle fell over. There was a box of Kleenex tissues on the nightstand and of course the top tissue caught fire. I was a stupid girl when it came to fire, so I ran with the lighted tissue to the open window.

In a futile effort to throw out the fire (we kept our windows open at night and/or during nap time) there was a breeze blowing the curtains inward, as I approached with the burning tissue in hand, the curtains caught fire. You already knew that this story would have some movement!

I panicked, ran to my door opened it and, with the fresh draft thus created, the flames seemed to lick all around the window, the curtains and the windowsill. I panicked, I yelled "ma chamber est en feu!" my room is on fire! Over and over again as I ran out of my room. I ran downstairs with my pet whippet, Nanny, and stood by the door to the outside. I was very frightened, but I didn't want to go out unless the whole house was going to burn. So I waited by the front door, yelling up toward the upstairs. "Est-ce que le feu est éteint?" Is the fire out? All the while, my mother, father, grandfather, my brother Pierre, aunt Gertrude and Marie Jeanne Brulé (a lady who lived with us) had formed a bucket brigade to douse the fire with every available kitchen pot filled with water. They just passed the water filled pots to one another like a chain gang, only this was the Lafond gang and they were moving at a fast pace. I came up to see what was happening because no one was speaking. I could not hear a sound coming from anyone. I saw my family struggling with those heavy pots filled with water.

Mother did not want to call the firemen who would destroy the house, that's why the bucket brigade was so efficient. After all, there was a Réveillon that night at our house and the fire hoses would ruin everything. That's faith, I believe, and a little bit of luck is more to the point.

One glimpse at what they were doing to put out the fire, and I ran back downstairs crying, terrified at what I had done and sure that the entire house would burn, if not the house at least my own bedroom. Actually it was a duplex. It never occurred to me that our neighbors might also be in danger.

My Dad came downstairs after what seemed an eternity of nervously waiting. He had come to fetch me and he carried me upstairs. As we passed my bedroom I wouldn't look inside my room, I was still shaking and terrified. I refused to look. My Dad was so gentle with me, so patient, still carrying me he walked inside my room in a slow measured step and turned slightly one way and then another to make sure I would see that the damage was not irreparable. Mostly the woodwork around the window, of course the curtains and a lot of smoke damage throughout the room. My father never once said, you know better than to play with matches or look at what can happen when you do…there was no scolding. His manner was comforting, he understood that I was devastated enough as it was.

We attended Midnight Mass as planned, the Réveillon took place after Mass and no one spent the night in my room. I shared Marie Jeanne's room the next few nights.

I did not play with matches ever again. I was truly traumatized and ashamed at what I had done, yet my intentions were such devout religious ones – perhaps for that reason we were spared…it's a good thought!

After the holidays the painters and workmen came to repair

the damage to my room. However, a fresh coat of paint never erased the trauma or the guilt I carried with me for some time. That was one very, very hard lesson learned.

Good wishes for the New Year

Leisurely investigating areas of Lac des Francais

Beautiful scene on Lac des Francais, Ste. Marcelline, Jolliette County, P. Quebec

Summer Camp Memories

Camp le Capitaine on the shores of Lac des Francais. As the camp brochure states: "The Camp aims to develop a physical personality that is healthy and alert and a moral personality with attributes of resourcefulness, of social matters, and balance. Everything needed in life. All this in a joyful holiday atmosphere. The activities are headed by a Committee made up of campers who are elected by all campers. Supervision exists without constraint, the counselors accompany the campers everywhere to make decisions and take charge when the unexpected presents itself."

In 1931, the year I was born, our father purchased a beautiful piece of land on the shores of Lac des Français, near the village of Ste. Marcelline in the County of Joliette in the Province of Québec in the heart of the Laurentians. There, father founded and directed a boys camp he named Camp Le Capitaine – father was a reservist in the Canadian Army.

Rodolphe Lafond taught Physical Education for a number of years before the camp came into being, so he had a wide group of young men from whom to offer a spot as counselor at Camp le Capitaine. French and English were spoken at the camp and the French speaking campers learned English and the English speaking campers learned French. It was a unique environment for young boys.

Camp Le Capitaine was located 55 miles from Montreal and only 13 miles from the county of Joliette. The closest village was Ste. Marcelline. Capitaine Lafond was a law graduate from the University of Montreal and he sought college students to become counselors at the camp. These young men attended the following Universities: University of Montreal, McGill University, Toronto University and the Military College in Kingston, Ontario.

During the time I spent at the camp, from the time I was ten days old, my parents had a log cabin on stilts where we slept during camp season. The season was July first to September first.

When my brother Pierre was old enough to join the other boys on the camp grounds, he shared their tents and bungalows, leaving the family bungalow behind. Being the son of the camp's owners, he was able to freely enjoy the considerable benefits that campers enjoyed during their summers. Who could have asked for a better succession of summer vacations?

There was a wonderful cook working at the camp named *Monsieur Lambert* who took me under his wing, allowing me free access to the kitchen and sometimes giving me special treats. My mother probably had an arrangement with M. Lambert to watch over me when I came down from our bungalow. My brother was able to blend in with the other campers and become one of them, but being a girl, often watching from the sidelines or spending time with M. Lambert, my life was a lot different from Pierre's.

Mr. Lambert was kind and gentle with me. I enjoyed spending time with him and I think, now, that perhaps he enjoyed my company too. When I was five or six, and came down to the kitchen, M. Lambert would prepare a *tartine*, a snack which consisted of one piece of bread with something on it. The bread was always freshly baked with homemade, healthy ingredients. Very much like the fresh bread mother bought at the small bakery in our neighborhood in Montreal.

M. Lambert took a piece of that good bread and, are you ready for this? He spread it with a generous layer of fresh sour cream and sprinkled *cassonade* on it – "Cassonade" is an old French word dating back to 1578 – it is simply brown sugar in French Canada! It was an afternoon snack and eating it was pure joy. I still treasure the memory of the tartine and time spent with M. Lambert. Fortunately for my arteries, those wonderful tartines existed only a brief time. Tastes change as do habits. It was awfully good, though.

One day Mr. Lambert decided to make me a very special present. He built a small log dollhouse out of half timbers. My Dad was probably in on the surprise and facilitated the acquisition of half timbers for the dollhouse.

It had two windows, a door, a small, built-in wooden bench inside, and a veranda. That was all it needed. I had my dolls' buggy inside and my dolls. I was proud of having my own playhouse at Camp le Capitaine; not that there was much competition for dollhouses in a camp full of boys.

My father's youngest sister, fresh out of nursing school at l'Hôpital Notre Dame in Montreal, came to work at Camp Le Capitaine for a couple of summers. So the count grew to three in the female contingent. Maman, Tante Gertrude and Suzanne.

Using one of the camp's electric crafting tools that burns lines and letters into wood, he christened his creation *"Villa Suzon,"* which was one of my nicknames. When your name is Suzanne you have access to several nicknames: *Suzon, Suzy, Suzette*. I answered to each of them.

I loved my dollhouse, and I didn't care if the campers looked at it a bit askance. I would be outside playing with my dolls, lost in my imaginary tea parties and housekeeping duties, and some of the younger campers would just look and pass on by. Fortunately, some of the camp counselors took time to stop and talk. It was fun to talk to them and I was thankful when the counselors included me in their conversations, I enjoyed their company. Initially I was a shy child, but somehow the exposure to camp life and the many activities in which I participated changed all that.

The camp is where I learned to swim, to dive, to properly paddle a canoe with a J-stroke, to row a boat – a "chaloupe", and even how to sail a dingy.

I had the run of the lake, not on my own, of course, but usually under the protective eye of my mother, or an older cousin or an adult counselor.

When I think back to those days, those memories paint a picture for me: Vivid summer colors, blue skies, blue water, white clouds, and I can also see sunny hiking trails that meandered through thick stands of pine trees.

Mother and I, and often one of her invited friends, be it a sister-in-law or a cousin, would love to go berry-picking. We sought out wonderful tiny strawberries, *fraises des bois*, that grew in the woods and were very sweet. We picked raspberries and also blackberries. The woods were filled with so many delicious options.

I can still picture my mother wearing her favorite berry-picking dress. She was a fine seamstress and had made the dress herself. It had a white background with bright red strawberries sprinkled throughout the cotton dress. I would always ask her to wear that specific dress whenever we went on our berry-picking expeditions. It too is now part of my treasured childhood memories.

We would carry small metal pails and follow the trails that Mother knew would lead us to the bushes with the most berries. Picking the berries with our own hands always made the eating that much better.

An Indian ceremony takes place during the summer (First Nation) with the Big Chief Capitaine Lafond, called 'Le Grand Manitou' and all campers are part of the Moukmouk tribe. There are special songs, rites and costumes. Visitors are always welcome and show up in big numbers on Sundays. Camp le Capitaine opens July 1st until September 1st. Cost is $18.00 per week, travel not included.

*Suzanne Lafond and cousin Judith Lafond
heading out under sail*

Sundays were visitors' days at The Captain's Camp. Although parents were welcome to visit anytime. Mostly they came Sundays in the afternoon, so it was a big day for the campers, the counselors, the staff and the visitors.

Early on Sundays, the campers would be instructed to go bathe in the lake, making sure to give special attention to washing their necks and behind their ears. Each camper had his own bar of soap, wash cloth and towel. The bathing area was in the shallow end of the lake, away from the deeper swimming area with the spring diving boards.

My father would position himself at the top of a gentle slope leading to the lake, dressed in his white flannel pants, white shirt with turned up cuffs, open neck and a pith helmet under his arm when he didn't have it on his head. He cut quite a figure. That was my dad. It wasn't an act, it was all very natural.

Peach Cobbler Stories

It was the Sunday Inspection! Father would inspect one camper after another, checking necks and behind the ears. Campers either passed or were sent back to the lake for an extra scrubbing to finish the job. I am quite sure, now that I have raised 3 sons, that the campers hated this ritual.

Also on Sundays, my mother, who hadn't been driving a car for very long at that time, was given an old Packard automobile by my Dad, which she named Emma. It was old when my father bought it. I thought it was grand with a running board, no less.

Mother's Sunday morning duty was to drive Emma into the next village to pick up the local priest who celebrated Mass for the campers and staff. This was an understanding my parents had with the parish at Ste. Marcelline, every year.

In the open air a time for prayer at Sunday Mass

Services were held in a tent with a very rudimentary wooden cross atop the main post. A table was the altar and seating was provided with folding chairs from the dining hall. If campers wanted to receive communion, they would put a small folded piece of paper, taken from one box into another, thus indicating to the priest how many hosts should be blessed.

After Mass, mother would drive the priest back to his parish, Ste. Marcelline, the nearest village.

I always enjoyed Catholic Mass on the campgrounds. I thought it was very appropriate. There is no doubt in my mind that it meant more to me than to my brother, Pierre, or the other campers.

When I first joined the younger campers, around age six and seven years old, I had already been coming to the camp for six summers. Of couse I had always been the only girl, it was a boys camp after all. I naturally stood out from the crowd, but I can honetly say that I intergrated easily and naturally. I played in the sandboxes and helped build castles and forts. I went on the same hikes the campers my age went on and did a lot of things available to six and seven year old campers at Camp Le Capitaine.

Around the age of ten or eleven, my parents allowed me to have my own private table in the dining room, so I didn't have to sit at the long tables filled with the boy campers.

I was also permitted to invite a guest to join me at my table, any time. Generally, I would ask one of the counselors to be my dining companion. Even then it seems I preferred the company of more mature guys! Those lunch dates were instructive for me and a nice way to spend mealtime.

We also had movie night once a week in the dining hall, and sometimes silhouette night, where counselors would make figures with their hands and cast the shadows from behind a large sheet, with lights behind them. They wrote skits and animated the characters with hand silhouettes, delighting everyone with their stories. Simple, but good fun always met with a great deal of laughter.

The movies often featured Charlie Chaplin and other silent film stars. There was something so comical about seeing The Little Tramp survive his various ordeals and sometimes find true love by the end of the reels. Everyone, young and old enjoyed movie night.

Another highlight of the week was when the canteen would open after one of the noon meals. This was the only time campers were allowed to purchase penny candy, chewing gum or chocolate bars. A line would form inside the dining hall and a counselor would assist Mother to write down the name of each camper and list exactly what sweets were purchased, so an accurate record could be given to parents at the end of camping season. Sweets were never a daily occurance either at home or at camp, so the same philosophy existed at Camp Le Capitaine.

The lake was beautiful and offered more enticements than just swimming, canoeing, rowing and sailing…and bathing.

Some nights, a few of the male counselors not on duty, would get into canoes after the sun went down, and sneak across the lake, which was only about a mile wide, to court young ladies who lived on the other shore. The following days, I would hear snippets of conversations among the counselors, and a bit of razzing from the campers, but I was never privy to those conversations. I believe I understood it was boy stuff much as my chats with my friends were "girl stuff.

*Dad's pet dog whose name has been forgotten.
The breed is a Russian Wolfhound.*

*Camp le Capitaine above the tents and bungalows –
Nature at its best. View of Lac des Français*

*For the very young campers there was
castle building in the sand.*

Pair of divers from the high board

Horse jumping was one of the activities for those qualified.

Pole Vaulting at Camp le Capitaine

*A small biplane a camper's father
landed on Lac des Français*

Papa with his pith helmet and cigar at Camp Le Capitaine

Framing the bungalows and tents is a thick forest on both sides of the gentle slope

The Lafond family bungalow on stilts

View of the dining room and kitchen

Across the lake were fields for riding, basketball, volleyball and badminton.

Peach Cobbler Stories

Five Beaver Pelts & Two Onyx Eyes

As with most children, summer was and is my favorite time of year. Growing up in Canada where winters are very long, summers appear sure of their welcome and so deserving. As children, we ran headlong to meet summer and held on to it until school began again in September.

My summers, the first thirteen specifically, were unlike any I ever heard of. You see, I had the dubious distinction of being the only girl in a boys summer camp. My father owned, operated and directed the only French Canadian boys camp in all of Canada. It was known as *Camp Le Capitaine*. It (the camp) and I saw the first light of summer the same year, 1931. It opened its gates on July 1 and I opened my eyes to the world on June 25th. I arrived at the camp without fanfare when I was ten days old and returned with my parents and older brother for the next twelve summers.

When I was of an age to follow the youngest group of campers in their rounds of daily activities, I was allowed to do so. I was tolerated if not accepted by my fellow campers; all boys, remember. With them I learned to swim, to dive, to paddle a canoe, to capsize it and find air space in its inverted hull in order to survive a dunking, to sail a dinghy, to ride horseback, to hike, in a word to do the things all children dream of doing and few are fortunate enough to do all summer long, year after year. How lucky I was!

There was so much going on all around me that my childhood recollections remind me of a Seurat canvas, where each dot is an adventure, an experience, a high point and collectively they reflect impressions of happy childhood summers.

My adventures were small ones, never life threatening ones, yet I remember them still.

The night, for instance, when there was an Indian Pow Wow around the campfire. Everyone was encircled about the fire in anticipation of the rare and special visit of a celebrated Indian Chief, who lived deep in the Canadian North. To the sound of tom-toms, the Chief arrived wrapped in a five point Hudson Bay blanket. The five parallel lines woven in contrasting wool in the Chief's blanket indicated that it had been exchanged for five beaver pelts. That made it a fine one indeed. The woven bars in the blanket were the price tag actually. Anyway, the great Chief talked of his tribe, of legends past, of the revered Manitou, a spirit in the sky who knew all, saw all and heard all. This wonderful Chief, who captivated all the campers with his Indian lore, was my father in feather headress, a little war paint and this beautiful Hudson's Bay blanket hanging from his broad shoulders. Such innocent rituals would be frowned upon in this day of more respect and understanding of First Nations. Looking back I must say, what was done and spoken had an aura of respect for our native Canadians, nothing pejorative was ever intended.

One of the counselors was part Indian and he carved a huge totem pole out of one of the camp's tree trunks. We saw it progress from a rough idea into a beautiful piece of art over weeks of intensive hand labor, eventually earning a place of honor at the campground.

After taps sounded that night, I had permission to sleep in the tent adjoining my parents bungalow with Judith, a visiting cousin my age and my dog, a whippet I called Nanny. We three slept soundly until Nanny left the tent to investigate something she heard. When she did not return immediately, I went out looking for her with my flashlight. I jumped into my slippers and took off looking like a wee ghost myself with my nightgown floating about my legs. I found Nanny growling at something a short distance from the tent. I flashed my light ahead and two shining eyes looked past the light at me. We stood motionless, Nanny, this animal I took to be a wolf, and me. Three creatures frozen in time. It seemed like hours before I got over the shock and fear finally propelled me. I took off like the wind, losing a slipper in my haste. I scampered up the bungalow steps to tell my parents about the wolf I had just seen. I described him in the most careful detail. My father then took my hand and together we went back to have a look at the wolf. I could see my little slipper where the wolf had been, but the wolf was gone by now. We woke up Judith and all of us spent the rest of the night in the bungalow, safe and secure from wolves with gleaming eyes.

The next day, there were reports circulating among staff, campers and counselors alike that a wolf-like creature had visited the camp and was last seen going over a hill and into the woods. I had not dreamed this after all. My young and always active imagination was not to blame this time.

Long after the incident had been forgotten by all, I took special pleasure in recalling my encounter with this creature with the piercing onyx eyes. No one ever knew for sure if indeed it had been a wolf, but to this day I can see the eyes beaming back my light, not in a menacing way, but every bit as curious about me as I was about him.

Strong, healthy young men make up the counselor corps

Peach Cobbler Stories

Maman being a good sport in a game of softball

Memories of My Mother

Her name was Léa Victoria Moquin Lafond. I have a very old memory of Mother and me on one of our shopping trips to "downtown" Montréal. We were both dressed in spiffy outfits – (in the day, circa mid-1930s, women spruced up to "go shopping downtown.") To be clear, both Mother and I loved "dressing up." We were going to do what shopping Mother needed, have lunch in one of the department store's Tea Room, and take a 'tramway' home after that. We were on the fourth floor of said department store and ready to leave. We lined up behind others to get on the elevator to the street level. Mother and I got separated, that is, I never got on the elevator.

When the elevator doors closed, there I was. A lost four year old! I looked around and a salesperson approached and asked me if I was lost. I answered her in French that I didn't get on the elevator with my mother. Someone else came along and picked me up and sat me on the counter. Very soon many sales people gathered, some spoke to me in French, others in English. I answered all their questions, in French or in English depending on the question posed. Then one English speaking sales lady asked me to describe my mother. I answered this way: "My mother looks like me!" You see, I had heard it said many times, by family friends or relatives "Léa, how like you she is!" Mother finally retraced her steps and found me holding court sitting on a countertop in the ladies' lingerie department.

My first recollection ever, and that is subject to scrutiny because I was nine months old and sleeping in a pram on our balcony. It was winter and it was thought that a baby swaddled in warm clothes would do well to breathe and nap in the cool (not frigid, of course) afternoon air.

I have seen a photo of the pram, with me in it, on the balcony, with snow garnishing the balcony rail. I question whether I really recall that or if seeing the photograph at a young age allowed me to "remember" that place, that time and that nap. I am not so sure!

When we still lived in Outremont - an apt name as the area was indeed on the side of Mount Royal. One day Mother was baking and needed a five pound bag of sugar. There was a small grocery store (those are called "dépanneurs" today), a short distance from our Outremont apartment. All that was necessary was for Mother to cross the street with me and I was to call back from across the street to have her come and escort me back to the side we lived on. I bought the sugar and put the five pound bag on my sled and proceeded to return to the spot across from our apartment. I stood there a couple of minutes calling out Maman! Maman! Soon Mother appeared and crossed the street with me. I could only cross the street if escorted by Mother or a visiting relative. When Mother picked up the bag of sugar after the ride on my sled, there was a hole in the bag and scarcely two or three pounds were left. Enough for Mother to finish her baking, but not what one would call a successful errand.

I thought my mother was very beautiful. Every time Mother asked me to pick up *Ladies' Home Journal* or *Good Housekeeping* when the new monthly editions came out, I did so. I bought the two magazines with money Mother had given me that morning. On the way home, at the end of the school day, I would purchase them.

I would look at the pretty ladies on the cover and think to myself that the photographs of the women were beautiful but MY mother was even more attractive. I was so proud of her.

Mother was gentle, but could be firm. We were very close. As I got older and spent time around boys, during whatever conversations we were having, I would often quote something my mother had taught me or told me about. I didn't realize, at the time, how often I did that until one day one of the boys asked me this: "Suzy, what does your mother think about such and such…?" When that happened a few more times, I got the message and stopped quoting my mother – much to everyone's relief, I imagine. We were in our teens, after all!

Mother did indulge me in many ways. I dare say I was a spoiled little girl, but more importantly, she wanted me to reach for things she wasn't offered and did not have growing up. I love singing childhood French songs and did so around the house when just Mother and I were home alone. She asked me once if I would like to take singing lessons. I wasn't so keen on doing that, but I wanted to learn to dance.

FRENCH FOLKLORIC SONGS OF MY YOUTH
A la Québécoise Meilleures
Chansons de Notre Folklore - Pierre Daignault

I grew up hearing French folkloric songs typical of the province of Québec that were sung, either on the radio or by family members and friends, but especially when we gathered. They are embedded in my brain. Some were sad, others quite funny, but all had a very easy melody for children to learn.

I cannot explain why any given song on any given year, decade or day, would enter my head. Nothing will chase them away, even now, until I give in and begin singing them.

Here, are some titles of those songs of my youth as a Québécoise:

A la Claire Fontaine, *(Passing by the Clear Fountain)*
A la Volette, *(A Bird in Flight Sings a Sad Song)*
Alouette, *(You know this song which plucks all the feathers from the lark)*
C'est l'aviron qui nous mène, *(The paddle takes us upstream…)*
Auprès de ma Blonde *(Near my beloved the song asks the young girl whose husband was taken by the Dutch what she would give to free him. She answers that she would give Versailles, Paris and St. Denis)*
En passant par la Lorraine *(Young girl, wearing clogs, reaches la Lorraine, a province in eastern France. And meets three capitaines…)*
Malbrough s'en va-t-en guerre *(Malborough is going off to war, he is killed in the war. We hear the sad news of his burial and the flight of the lark from the rose bush next to his beloved. Everyone witnessed Malbrough's soul fly away.)*

There are dozens more. Fortunately I have a book of these French and Canadian songs and I refer to it for the words that I cannot resurrect.

Suzanne
May 2013

Very soon I was enrolled in dance school to learn ballet. This was pre-school, but I did not pursue it, sorry to say, once I entered first grade. If nothing else, it gave me an early appreciation for ballet which I admire and love to this day.

Many years ago, it was early August 1969, my sister-in-law, Anne Rosevear Lafond, Pierre Lafond's wife, and their four children were visiting Nashville for ten days. That increased my household by five, for a total of eleven, including my mother, Léa Moquin Lafond, who had moved to Nashville in 1962. So, for nearly two weeks, I hosted eleven people for dinner every night.

Mother generally brought the main course, and I did the rest. It was hectic, but fun. One of the last meals we had was very special because Mother was leaving the next day for a trip to Montreal to visit friends and relatives. Also leaving the next day were Anne Lafond and her four children: Lise Anne, David, Michelle and Denise.

Mother first went by way of Windsor, Ontario to visit family friends, Mr. and Mrs. Joe Mencel. Then on to London, Ontario to visit my father's brother, Lucien Lafond and his family.

For some reason, I wanted the last evening for our visitors to be the bon voyage dinner for Mother, for Anne Lafond, my nieces and nephew: Lise Anne, David, Michelle and Denise to be extra special. We had a lovely time at dinner. The adults drank a little wine and the children had a good time co-mingling with their cousins. After dinner, Mother helped me clear the table and collect everyone's napkins (serviettes, as we call them in Canada) and table cloth. Briefly, Mother and I found each other in the laundry room putting everything in the washing machine for next day's laundry.

Mother stopped to take both of my hands into hers. We were a little flushed from drinking one-half a glass of wine (neither of us drank very much at all, when we did drink). We looked at one another face to face, holding each other's hands, and she said this: "I am so proud of you, there is nothing you cannot do, and whatever you do, you do beautifully." We became tearful and we hugged. Then I said this to my mother: "Maman, je suis comme je suis grâce a toi c'est toi qui m'a montré comment faire toutes choses." I translate: "I am who I am because of you. You are the one who taught me how to do all things."

Neither one of us could have known that those were to be the very last words spoken between us. My mother was killed in an automobile accident on her way to Montreal from London, Ontario. She had been urged to travel by car with my father's sister and her son, who happened to arrive on the scene at my uncle Lucien's house.

Those last words were of some comfort to me at this tragic time. Mother was only 69 years old. Forty-four years later that moment in my laundry room, is etched in my heart and there it will stay for as long as I live. Not a day goes by that I do not think of my mother and father. I had so much more to say to her, some regrets at not having more time for her after she moved to Nashville. The words wouldn't change anything…sad to say. I hope she knows that now.

The boys being photographed with the girls looking on. Pierre is next to Bill Shatner, the acclaimed actor. Suzanne and Pierre lived at 4403 Marcil Ave. Bill lived at 4407 and Seymour, the other seated boy, lived at 4405.

*Pierre Lafond school photo while at
Lower Canada College (High School)*

Print job in Montreal for Chase & Sanborn Coffee. A watercolor sketch based on a portrait of Suzanne was used instead of her headshot. Circa 1950

Peach Cobbler Stories

Nominees representing their football teams from across Canada, circa 1952. Suzanne is second front left.

Photo shoot and feature story about Suzanne in connection with the Alouette team playing in the Grey Cup Finals

Peach Cobbler Stories

Suzanne is on the back seat of the convertible while her maman is sitting in the passenger seat. The car is surrounded by fans who never left their posts as the parade slowly traveled the course. They sang "Alouette gentil alouette," over and over again. It was a fun day!

Capitaine Lafond putting Rath Patrick through Dressage paces at home on Clanranald in front of the horse barn and the indoor manège

Rodolphe Lafond and his mount Rath Patrick going through their paces in a competition representing Canada

My Father's Journey to the Olympics

My father grew up on a farm in Drummond county, in the village of *Saint Majorique*, in the Eastern Townships.

He was one of eleven children, though one sibling died at birth.

My grandfather was named Benoit Lafond and Dad's mother was Ernestine Trudel Lafond. Benoit owned a beautiful farm where my father grew up with all his brothers and sisters.

He didn't choose to become a farmer. So after grammar school and high school, he enrolled in a Seminary where he trained to become a priest. He received a fabulous education, learning Greek, Latin and Philosophy, a fine classical education as it is called. This was in anticipation of becoming a man of the cloth, though he subsequently decided not to follow that path. He excelled academically. Later he attended The University of Montreal, where he studied law.

When he graduated from law school, he didn't pass the bar exam on his first try. While he could have taken the exam again and again, times were hard because it was at the height of the Great Depression, as it became known. That was in 1929-30. Job prospects were bleak. Instead, he became very involved in sports, and found a job as athletic director at the University of Montreal, a position he held for 13 years. During this time, one of his major achievements was introducing Canadian/American style football to Canadian colleges, even playing on the University of Montreal team before finishing college.

My mother had a funny cartoon of a football team pileup and underneath on the very bottom was number 13. We were told it was in tribute to my dad's playing efforts. I suspect that might have just been a family joke that was told over the years.

He began teaching physical education at other private French schools throughout the area, developing a reputation for excellence in the field.

All the while he nurtured his love of horse-back riding, studying with a French-Canadian instructor named *Monsieur Langlois,* who was very schooled in the fine art of dressage.

We left NDG and our Dad bought a house on *Clanranald*. The home was a two-story house with an orchard and an old barn. My dad turned the front of the barn into the family garage, and made the side of the barn into an indoor riding manège, permitting him to ride year-round, even in the brutally cold Canadian winters, protected from the snow and deep-freeze. This was extremely important for a sport like dressage, which depended on having complete control of your mount at all times, with a regular practice schedule. There was an outdoor "piste" or trail which skirted around the apple trees in the orchard. That trail was used during good weather.

Unlike soring, sometimes used in the training of Tennessee Walking Horses, dressage requires finesse to teach the high stepping of the horse with only the calf of the legs and the reins. It is called La Haute Ecole or high schooling of the horse. I think my dad was something of an early version of The Horse Whisperer, able to control the movements of his horses with the flex of the calves of his legs and slight pressure from the hands as he held the reins.

He became very good at dressage, competing in international equestrian events, including the Pan-American Games in Mexico City.

Years later, after my parents divorced, Dad moved to Santa Barbara, California specifically to be close to the training facilities of the United States Equestrian Team. At the time, my father was the solo member of the Canadian Equestrian Team, so he wanted to train with people of similar skills and abilities, who were practicing dressage riding as he was.

That is how my family came to Santa Barbara, where my brother Pierre still lives and has found a meaningful life for himself and his own family as a very successful wine maker (Santa Barbara Winery wines and Lafond Wines & Vineyards), restaurateur, businessman and community leader.

In 1956 my father represented Canada in the 16th Summer Olympics. While the majority of the track and field events were held in Melbourne, Australia, the equestrian events were held in Stockholm, Sweden due to quarantine regulations in Australia that were far too stringent for a performing animal, such as a horse trained in dressage.

He was the only person in all of Canada representing Canada in the Dressage event at the Olympics. Never mind that he was a Canadian team of one. He was there having paid his own way for himself and Rath Patrick, his horse. He had come to Stockholm, Sweden from Santa Barbara, CA. The adventures he had transporting his horse across, first in the US from Santa Barbara to New York and from NewYork across the ocean is a tale that would take up far too much time. Let it be known that he had more than one great challenge. I still don't know why he never gave up. Lesser men would have!

I have an old film on celluloid where our father can be seen riding Rath Patrick in the opening ceremonies at the Equestrian Event in Stockholm. He is seen riding immediately after the Queen of England. Queen Elizabeth is in a horse-drawn carriage. Father sent us duplicates of the film taken in Stockholm. How proud he must have felt. I was very proud of him too. He didn't win any medals, but what he accomplished, in my view, is far more impressive. A One Man Team, he was reaching for a life-long dream with difficulties at every turn. As for me, I maintain that he won his own special medal by reaching his nearly impossible dream.

Capitaine Lafond and Major Henri de Reverony Saint–Cyr, one of the elite riders of Le Cadre Noir de Saumur, Bretagne. Cadre Noir refers to the color of the horses. They are all black.

Rodolphe Lafond: His Story

"You must come" Pierre said.

"I will. Soon...I'll plan a visit," I said.

"You don't understand, Suzanne, you should come right away."

It sounded urgent, I hadn't thought that our father's illness was serious. He had a lingering cough for two or three months and the doctor had recommended surgery. There was no way to diagnose a shadow on one of his lungs without opening up the chest and exploring.

This was 1959 and medicine had not advanced to what is known today. There are better and safer choices to be made today when confronted with a shadow on a person's X-rays.

I made hurried arrangements to have someone care for my two young sons. Marc was three years old and Christian only nine months old. Two days after Pierre's phone call I was in Santa Barbara. Pierre met me at the plane and took me immediately to our father's bedside at Cottage Hospital.

"Pops," as we called father, was pleased to see me, I felt it. "You've come to my funeral, Sis?" He said in an attempt at lightheartedness. "I've come to see you because Pierre said you were sick, but you don't look sick to me, Pops," I teased.

The doctors had taken father off the blood thinning medication – medication he had been given following a mild heart attack. There might be a wait of ten days to two weeks before the surgery would be scheduled, a lung examination as it were.

While the doctors, father and I waited for the surgery, I spent every morning and lunch at Cottage hospital. For Pops and I, those were wonderful days of catching up with one another's lives. The nurses even brought me a lunch tray when they brought food to my father. I left after lunch each day, to give Pops a chance to have a nap and returned later in the day.

Ten days after my arrival in Santa Barbara, father had surgery. The shadow on his lung was a tumor, but a benign tumor. How grateful we all were at the news. The nurses on father's floor danced around with me outside his room, in the hallway. The nurses and I were so relieved when we heard the good news. Father had charmed the nurses at the hospital much as he charmed most women he met.

I was there, in his room, when they returned father from the Intensive Care Unit. I looked into his ashen face and blurted out that he did not have cancer, that he would be fine and that I loved him. Father had talked of his trip to Saumur, in the spring and his plan to take me with him to see Saumur and meet some of the riders he knew there. Saumur was a dressage riding mecca among its many attributes.

A few hours later I boarded a plane to Nashville, to rejoin my husband and two small sons. It was the week before Christmas and there was much to do, plus I missed my little boys terribly. How different the flight back to Nashville was as compared to the one taking me to California ten days earlier. I carried the weight of anxiety, bewilderment and sadness on that earlier journey. This one was full of happy anticipation.

I landed in Nashville and was greeted by my husband, Kermit, and a telephone page at the airport. The paged message asked me to call Pierre as soon as possible. I knew then, what the news would be. Father had died. He had suffered a pulmonary embolism just a few hours after I left. I was probably over the Grand Canyon when he died.

Pierre and I talked. He said not to come back. "You were here when it mattered. Stay with your husband and your babies. That's where you need to be." He was right, of course.

I did not go back for his funeral. Father was cremated and his ashes scattered in the Pacific Ocean. We had a sad Christmas that year, but I had the comfort of motherhood to distract me from my sadness, yet grateful for the ten days spent with Pops before he had surgery. One of the things he said to me during my visit was this: "I've always thought you demonstrated good judgment, Sis."
That was an important statement for me to hear.

Just when in his life my father decided to become a dressage rider, I am not sure. It seems it might have been during the years of Camp le Capitaine. Around that time, father met a Monsieur Langlois who was a well known dressage rider. They became friends and the idea of getting into dressage in a serious way was born in Rodolphe. Dressage is often referred to as the "High Schooling" (La Haute Ecole) of the horse. I will attempt to explain in the simplest terms what I learned talking to my father and reading some of his books on dressage.

Dressage is a philosophy, a methodology in schooling a horse. It recognizes that the horse has three learning centers: Motor, Emotional (sensations) and Intellectual (understanding, memory and the will). The dominant notion in schooling a horse is in recognizing that the natural equilibrium of the horse is destroyed by the presence of a rider on his back. The beginning step in dressage is to restore this equilibrium to the horse in motion.

The dedicated dressage student knows and understands the horse's anatomy. In time, the horse will respond to signals given to him with pressure from the rider's legs. There are other signals with the hands, the reins and sometimes with a riding crop. An accomplished dressage rider is in full control of himself and his mount at all times. It is a complicated, technical and serious discipline.

I have thought so much of my dad's story in the intervening years. He was a remarkable man and I have always thought his story needed to be told. It is a story of setting goals, hard work, great focus, perseverance, of reaching goals and then of dying.

Petit Souvenir de Papa

Mon Suzon,

Demain je partirai, bientôt sera ton tour,
Dans ce trop court trajet, c'est moi qui te précède,
Cependant sache bien, mignon petit amour,
Que toujours ton papa, avec tendresse observe
Le chemin que tu prends. Je vois tes beaux cheveux
Qui laissent sur ta route une blonde trainée,
Ton corps si fragile, tes membres gracieux…
Tout ça ne suffit pas sit tu veux être aimée.
Veux-tu savoir comment, veux-tu savoir pourquoi
L'on se fait des amis qui jamais ne nous laissent?
"Souris à l'Univers et le monde est à toi,"
Donne à bon escient des preuves de tendresse
Souris à l'avenir, il est plein de promesses.

Pops

This poem was written in my book of Autographs. A big trend among school girls when I was 11 to 14 circa 1942-1945. I have a few entries, but I treasure this one the most from my Papa.

A Poem From My Father

Translation from French

Tomorrow, I will be leaving (this earth),
soon will be your turn,
On this too brief a journey, I will precede you.
However, please know, dear love,
That always, your papa tenderly observes
The path you take. I see your beautiful hair
As it leaves behind a blond streak,
Your fragile body, your graceful limbs…
All that is not enough if you want to be loved.
Would you like to know how, and why we make friends
That will never leave us?
"Smile and the world smiles with you"
Give advisedly evidence of your tenderness,
Smile to the future, it is full of promise.

Pops

Peach Cobbler Stories

Photo taken in Bermuda to send to Kermit. He asked more than once for a photo and finally Suzanne asked someone from the Princess Hotel to take a photo for her. Her friends worked in a different part of the island and their path didn't cross that often.

How I Met Kermit

I am not sure if Marc, Christian and Eric ever knew the details of how I met their father. Kermit would smile when people asked us how we met. Kermit would defer to me to tell the story.

My friend, Anne Shirley Rosevear, became my sister-in-law a few years later, having married my brother Pierre. Anne and her friend, Jennifer Porteous had recently graduated from Nursing School at the same time. Anne and Jennifer had nursing jobs awaiting them in Bermuda at the Royal Victoria Hospital (if memory serves). They asked me to come to Bermuda with them. Of course 1 was tempted, but I would have to look for a job once there. I had a small nest egg saved up for a return flight from Montreal to Bermuda, but not much more for a life in Bermuda. Anne and Jenny stayed in the nurses' quarters near the hospital and I found a nice old house with a lovely old couple who ran a bed and breakfast business in their home. I liked them and their old place very much. So this was to be my little home in Bermuda for a while.

Anne called on the telephone to tell me that there was a to be a dance at the Naval Base that coming Saturday and that there would be a busload of nurses attending. She asked if I would like to join them. I told her as nicely as I could that "I didn't go to dances on a bus!" She was fine with that.

As it turned out, that very Saturday morning I had a job interview at the Coral Beach Club, one of Bermuda's finest resorts. I went to the interview. I could tell the gentleman who interviewed me was searching around in his mind to find a job he could offer. Finally he said I sure wish I had something better to offer you because I would like you to be part of our organization, but unfortunately I only have a need for chamber maids. I thanked him, and at the risk of coming off a bit too big for my breeches, I told him that I just couldn't accept a job in Bermuda that I wouldn't be proud to have at home. In other words, I wouldn't be a chamber maid in my city of Montreal. He was kind and told me he understood.

Before going to my "mobilette" and back home to the B & B, I decided to look around the beautiful grounds at the Coral Beach Club. I found a stone wall parapet that gave a splendid view of the ocean: The brochures talk about the pink beaches and the turquoise sea. It truly was so! I lost myself in the restful sight and lingered a few minutes. When I turned to leave, I was surprised to see a gentleman in a naval uniform sitting alone at one of the wrought iron tables. When I passed his table he commented on the view and he then proceeded to ask me to join him for a ginger ale or lemonade. I accepted. We talked a few minutes, then out of the blue, he told me there was a dance at the naval base that night and would I like to go? I told him I had heard that there was, and I accepted his invitation. I gave him my address and he said "Great I will see you tonight at six"

To my surprise, at six o'clock sharp, I saw through the front window a beautiful dark green Rolls Royce with the Admiral Seal on the front doors and a chauffeur getting out of the car to open the door for my date. His name was Lieutenant Murrell Bright, Admiral's Aid. I introduced him to Mr. and Mrs. Frith who owned the B & B. The Frith's and I had been peering through the lace curtains waiting for my "date" to arrive. Imagine their surprise and mine to see this elegant carriage taking me to the ball!

We arrived at the naval base and Murrell proceeded to bring me a drink and to introduce me to a few officers around the bar. After a short time, someone came to whisper something in Murrell's ear and he quickly turned to me and excused himself. When he returned, he told me that Admiral Spike Fahrion was ill - he added that he was drunk and throwing up.

Before he left, Murrell made sure I was not alone. He went to speak to Kermit C. Stengel, Jr. Lieutenant, JG (Junior Grade) and asked Kermit to take me under his wing and see me home. He did and we had a marvelous time getting to know one another. Kermit's flagship with Admiral Spike Fahrion was shipping out at six o'clock the next morning.

Kermit had been introduced to me as Casey Stengel actually K.C., so that is what I called him. It was later that I learned his full name. He asked me to stay up with him until he shipped out at six. So we did; we sat on a bench somewhere near a restaurant and continued this wonderful time of two people discovering one another's thoughts, backgrounds, and briefly our life experiences, until it was time to take me home and for him to get on board ship. We were two young people on the threshold of real love.

The mail from Newport, Rhode Island and Bermuda carried our letters daily. What an exciting time. Soon, Casey invited me to visit him in Newport. After thoughtful consideration and letters to my parents, I decided to leave Bermuda after a stay of only three months and go back home to Montreal.

I did return to Montreal and Casey invited me to visit him at the Naval base in Norfolk, Virginia. It was all done properly with Casey getting permission from my mother and father. He explained that Pat Noonan, a shipmate, was also inviting his girlfriend to Norfolk at the same time. Julie and I would share a room, so our parents were assured that all would be on the up and up.

What fun we all had. Julie and I did some shopping together while the boys were working. We went into a shoe store to try on shoes. When the young salesman approached us, he looked at the shoes I was wearing and he said: "Would you dig those crazy red shoes!" They really were very cute shoes, but they were red with just a little heel and a tiny red leather flower on the front of the shoe.

Julie and I spent the rest of our visit with our boyfriends saying: "Would you dig those crazy red shoes." Silly fun all four of us had.

We all got along so well.

Months later, Casey came to visit me in Montreal. I showed Kermit a little of the city - sightseeing here and there. One afternoon we stopped in a soda shop for ice cream. We sat at the counter and I ordered an ice cream soda and Kermit ordered a pint of ice cream. Not a dish, not a cone, not a sundae, but the boxed pint which he proceeded to eat with great gusto! That was an ice cream lover if I had ever seen one. Feeling a tad embarrassed for Kermit eating his pint out of the box, I looked around the soda shop and no one was looking or cared what we were doing.

Photo of the bride-to-be at home, moments before leaving for the church, Notre Dame des Neiges, January 9, 1954

The bride and her two beautiful bridesmaids at the foot of the stairs at the Ritz Carlton Hotel in Montreal. From left: Anne Shirley Rosevear and Marlene Grant, January 9, 1954

The newly married couple leaving the church, bracing for the cold Canadian late afternoon weather on January 9, 1954

Formal portrait of Suzanne in her wedding dress

The wedding couple on the stairs at the Ritz Carlton Hotel where the wedding reception took place. If the flowers look sad, they are, because it was 17 degrees below zero F. that day. When Suzanne's father opened the front door at home to take Suzanne and her family to church, the gardenias turned a light ivory color which matched her ivory-colored wedding dress. They were, in fact, fresh frozen.

Because of antiquated laws in the Catholic Church, certainly in Quebec province, if one of the people to be married was not Catholic, the wedding could not take place in the church proper. Because of this ruling, which no longer exists, Kermit, Suzanne their respective families and bridesmaids were relegated to the Sacristy. Very brief wedding vows were read to the couple by a priest who only spoke English with great difficulty, and then the registry was signed by bride and groom. There was no ceremony. It was too bad, but at least the couple was legally married. This ruling is no longer followed in Quebec or the USA. Photo taken on Wedding Day, January 9, 1954 at Notre Dame des Neiges (Our Lady of the Snows).

The wedding party, pictured left to right: Betsy Stengel, Kermit Stengel's sister, Suzanne's mom, Léa Lafond, Suzanne's dad, Rodolphe Lafond, Suzanne Lafond Stengel, Kermit Stengel, Marlene Grant, bridesmaid, Ann Rosevear, bridesmaid, Kermit Stengel, Sr., and Kermit's mother, Sara Sudekum Stengel.

After the wedding ceremony, Kermit and Suzanne are pictured heading to the wedding reception at the Ritz Carlton Hotel in Montreal.

Peach Cobbler Stories

*Suzanne standing in front of her new house
in progress at 4415 Gerald Place, in Belle Meade.
Photo taken in the Spring of 1969.*

Where did Grand-Daddy and I live?

Kermit C. Stengel, Jr. and I married in Montreal, in the Sacristy of the church. Because Kermit was a non-Catholic, we could not be married in the church. Remember that was January 9, 1954 and the rules about "mixed marriages" were frowned upon in the Catholic church in Catholic Québec, Canada. The church was Notre Dame des Neiges, Montreal – Our Lady of the Snows.

That is all changed at this writing. (January 2013). The changes occurred some years ago, in Québec. The US Catholic church was not that rigid in 1954, and certainly is not now.

Kermit and I honeymooned in Miami, Florida at the Sea View Hotel in the elegant penthouse owned by the senior Kermit Stengels. Afterward, we rented an apartment in Philadelphia, PA. while Kermit was enrolled at the Wharton School of Business and we lived on Chestnut Street.

Kermit's first job was as a Financial Analyst in Cleveland, Ohio. Neither Kermit nor I liked Cleveland very much. For one thing, we didn't see the sun from November until April.

However, we were delighted to welcome Marc Kermit Stengel while we lived in Cleveland (1.10.1956) – was it The Maternity Hospital at the Western Reserve? Not so sure of the Maternity Hospital's complete name.

Kermit really wanted to return to Nashville and possibly make a move to buy The Crescent Company, the family owned theatre business. We came to Nashville when Marc was six months old and stayed with the Stengels on Curtiswood Lane next to the Governor's Mansion.

Soon thereafter we set out in search of a house.

We found a ranch house at 888 Robertson Academy Road. It filled our needs as we raised our family. For it was there that Christian Sudekum Stengel (3.28.1959) and Eric Lafond Stengel (7.10.1961) were born. We lived on Robertson Academy Road for twelve years.

In the Fall of 1968, Kermit and I took steps to build a house for our growing family. I found an available lot on Gerald Place in Belle Meade – a short street between Jackson Boulevard and Belle Meade Boulevard. It was a beautiful three acre lot.

Kermit looked at the lot after I described it and he thought it would be a very nice place to build our home. Kermit worked with Belle Meade zoning to record the sale as two lots, in case some day, we might either want to build another house on the land or if it were sold it would enhance the value.

Kermit then asked me to think of a French name for the extension of the driveway which would serve 2 homes as a private access. I came up with Belle Terre (Beautiful Land) with a bow to Belle Meade.

The house was completed in the spring of 1969 and we moved in. It was so exciting to have a bigger and much handsomer house than we had known as a family. There were many happy years spent there.

Kermit and I officially divorced in March of 1981. It was wrenching to leave part of my life in Nashville, but something had to change for us. I headed for Santa Barbara where my brother Pierre has live since 1956.

Marc, Christian and Eric where not living in Nashville when their father and I were going through divorce proceedings.

Peach Cobbler Stories

*Portrait of Suzanne in 1980,
By her sweet and dear friend, Ann Street.*

*Five tennis dress designs to launch
"Tennis Fashions by Suzanne"*

Tennis Fashions by Suzanne in 1969

When my children were in preschool, I was amused by their drawings, along with those of their classmates. I was given a kiln at that time by a relative, Marie Sudekum Woolwine, who was a very fine artist, and I duplicated the children's artwork and transferred them onto ceramic tiles to give to their parents. That was an exploration of what I could do with creative tools, and while I didn't develop many additional applications with the gifted kiln, it did get my creative juices flowing.

In the mid 60s, Esty Foster, Headmaster of Ensworth School asked me if I would be willing to replace the French teacher who was headed to Switzerland with her husband. I accepted the offer with some temerity for this was my first teaching job. It turned out to be such a wonderful opportunity that I wondered why I hadn't gone into that profession much earlier. It was a job I loved and held for three years.

My husband, Kermit and I then decided to build our dream home in Belle Meade. This enormous task required my full-time attention. I saw the project as a once in a lifetime opportunity for our family. Ground-breaking took place in the Fall of 1968.

In August 1969, my mother was killed in a car accident in Canada on a roadtrip with relatives from Ontario to Montreal. Mother had come to live in Nashville in 1962. In August of 1969, she decided to visit family relatives in Canada. Her sudden death was very traumatic and tragic.

At the time of my mother's death, we had been planning a business project together. I was going to design a line of tennis dresses and she was going to make the sample prototypes. She was a wonderful dressmaker, having made her own dresses and mine for decades. Had she chosen to, she could have easily been a professional seamstress. People were always complimenting her on her work and tailoring skills. Her enthusiasm for the line of tennis dresses idea was a big part of my motivation to take on this new venture with her.

With her tragic death, I was not only without a mother, but without my dear and trusted partner in the enterprise. For a very brief time I considered shelving our plan, adding the idea to a list of dreams to be worked on at a later time. But as I reflected on my personal grief and stunning sense of loss, it became clear to me that continuing with our tennis dress project would be a fitting tribute to Mother, her creative skills and her support, and perhaps therapeutic for me.

I launched "Tennis Fashions by Suzanne" in honor of my mother, and proceeded to develop a line of sketches visualizing my designs.

I took a trip to New York City to visit a fabric library some of my contacts had told me about. It wasn't open to the general public, and required making an appointment, after which one was assigned an escort to be shown around the immense facility. Giving them some preliminary information as to what I was looking for, they were able to narrow the choices for me. I would have been lost without this escort's guidance. My plan was to make five samples to show to prospective buyers, and then start manufacturing dresses for orders I hoped would soon be forthcoming, to be filled by yours truly.

I selected white fabrics that were washable, easy care, something appropriate for sports activities. Time spent in the fabric library helped me narrow the choices out of far too many possibilities.

Once I had decided on the five styles for the tennis dresses, a wonderful, talented friend turned my rough sketches into fine drawings, then drew and cut patterns for each design.

It was time to select a dress manufacturer who would be willing to take on my orders. Again, by doing some networking, I heard that Tanner of North Carolina, in Rutherfordton, NC might be willing to contract with me to manufacture the tennis dresses. Tanner of Rutherfordton was owned by two brothers.

They made a pretty line of their own dresses, featuring Peter Pan collars which were quite popular with young women, wives and young mothers.

I traveled to Rutherfordton and took my ideas to the brothers and showed them sketches and patterns of the designs.

We signed a production contract and I was on my way. Even though they had their own line of dresses, my order with my label "Tennis Fashions by Suzanne" provided additional revenue for their company. Soon, I was receiving regular UPS shipments of the tennis dresses in wardrobe boxes, ready for me to begin placing them in retail outlets.

The tennis dresses were shipped to my house in Belle Meade, which was most definitely not zoned for commercial enterprises. Keep in mind that this was long before the concept of home businesses, emails, the Internet, or even cell phones. My neighbors had no idea I was running my fledging tennis fashion company out of my basement.

With the five designs and in various sizes, I flew to New York City to approach one of the leading fashion retailers, the highly acclaimed Saks Fifth Avenue, about carrying my line of tennis dresses. I was hoping to talk with one of the buyers in the active sportswear department.

I called the store and asked to speak to a buyer in active sportswear. I told the receptionist that I was from Nashville, Tennessee and in New York to give Sak's the opportunity of looking at my new line of tennis dresses. The buyer got on the phone and asked me if I could come in the afternoon. I told her I could, she set the time and I took a cab carrying the five tennis dresses and was on my way. The buyer was very receptive and said she liked the tennis dresses very much. She then decided on just two of the designs with the stipulation that they would have to carry the Sak's label. I was fine with relinquishing the Tennis Fashions by Suzanne for the Sak's label. Who wouldn't be?

Outside of Sak's, all other sales I made would carry the label Tennis Fashions by Suzanne. I was very excited, if you must know! It gave me bragging rights when selling to other stores and a sense of satisfaction to receive an order from Sak's Fifth Avenue. I saw it as a win, win transaction.

I flew back to Nashville, went to my basement where the tennis fashions were warehoused and put together the sizes and designs Saks had ordered, shipping their order by UPS back to Saks Fifth Avenue in New York.

Soon those dresses were being displayed in many of Saks Fifth Avenue stores around the country, giving me exposure from coast to coast, as it were. Not as Tennis Fashions by Suzanne, but with Saks Fifth Avenue's own label in the dresses I designed. I felt good about that.

I had no idea that selling to Sak's would be difficult at the time. I was told by a few people that this rarely happened, if ever, to anybody I knew in the design or manufacturing business. I had heard how some designers and sales reps spent years trying to cultivate a relationship with Sak's buyers to no avail. What had seemed like a logical progression to me, turned out to be a little out of the ordinary. Beginners' luck, perhaps.

I didn't have to pay to attend trade shows. I didn't have to buy ads in fashion magazines. I didn't have to work through anyone. There was just me, a one woman operation working from designing to selling. I had 5X7 cards made duplicating the sketches my friend had drawn, stapled a small sample of the fabic on each card as well as the colored trim on the ones with trim, and mailed them in professional envelopes with my company's name on them. I had drawn up a growing list of potential buyers. The cards and fabric samples were simple, but they caught some people's eye!

Models wearing Suzanne's tennis dresses for local newspaper feature

I was often asked how I had been able to place the tennis dresses in Sak's, in New York. The question baffled me a little. A touch of naïveté I suppose. My response was always the same: "I didn't know it couldn't be done." I wasn't being cheeky, just honest.

Back in Nashville, I found a way of mentioning that Sak's had given me an order for the Tennis Dresses by Suzanne as I called on local merchants in an attempt to sell my wares! If they were good enough for Saks Fifth Avenue, they just might be good enough for places like the Belle Meade Country Club Tennis Shop. And they were. However, I really didn't toss the Sak's name indiscriminately everywhere I went. Honest!

I got busy sending order forms with the sketches and fabric samples stapled to the sketches, to tennis shops and fashion retailers all over the country.

Keep in mind that this was in 1969, and I was making my way on my own without any fashion or retail experience. There wasn't a guideline for me to follow, and the rulebook had yet to be written. I just used what seemed to be common sense, the designs and my approach seemed to worked for me.

One day I stopped in at Rich-Swartz, a high-end women's clothing store with a couple of outlets in Nashville, to see how they were doing with their inventory of tennis dresses. The buyer gave me a status report, and then asked me if I had time to meet another supplier they worked with. She introduced me to a salesman who handled several lines of active sportswear. In my presence, the Rich-Swartz buyer told him of my recent success with Saks Fifth Avenue. I told him that I'd started my company a few months earlier, stored the inventory of Tennis Fashions by Suzanne in my home basement in Belle Meade, flew to New York City, called up Saks Fifth Avenue, went to see the active sportswear buyer who placed an order for the tennis dresses, and she told me the tennis dresses would be placed in various Saks stores across the country. As mentioned earlier, they would carry the Sak's label in each dress.

You should have seen the raised eyebrows and the questioning look on this man's face. He then told me that he had unsuccessfully spent thirteen years just trying to get an appointment with Saks Fifth Avenue, "a foot in the door," he said.

What was my secret? Who did I know? Was there a secret password?

Many times some people discourage you with their comments, but one has to proceed when you have a strong sense of certainty and you hope for a positive outcome. There is no magic, no secret, no password. A little drive and a good idea? Yes!

Family photo taken in the back yard of our first home at 888 Robertson Academy Road. From the left: Marc, Kermit, Suzanne, Christian, and Eric sitting on the grass.

Portrait of Christian, Marc and Eric Stengel, painted by Ann Street in 1969 under the bent, living, climbing tree, on Gerald Place. A favorite tree to all the residents of 4415 Gerald Place.

Newspaper society photo for Furbelows and Fanfare, a fundraiser for the Florence Crittenton Home for Unwed Mothers. Suzanne was President of the Junior Board of Florence Crittenton Home at the time of the photo.

Bath time with the Stengels

This is the original photo of the Stengel sons taken by their father when the family lived on Robertson Academy Road. Eric is five and a half months old, Christian is two years old, and Marc is five years old. The photo was taken in December 1961. The later version with the three brothers recreating their toboggan style pose is below.

More Christmas joy for Eric, Marc and Chris

Another Christmas at 888 Robertson Academy Road: Suzanne and the boys opening gifts from Santa Claus. Kermit is taking the photo.

New steel tennis racket for Suzanne from Kermit and the boys on Christmas morning

Christian's Christmas loot!

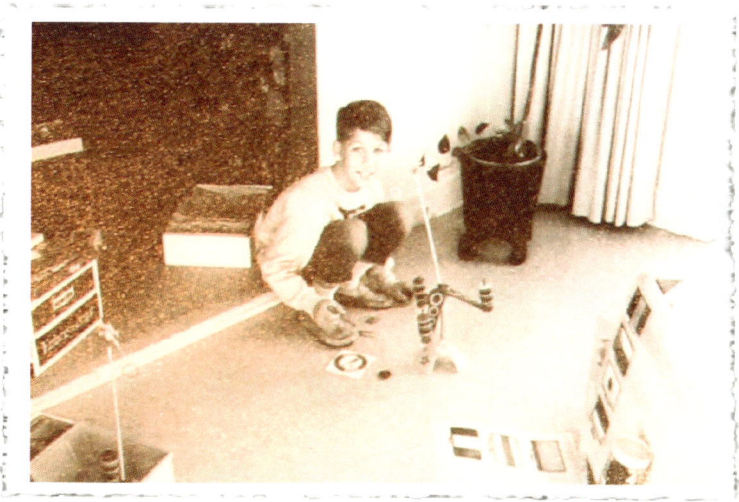

Marc's Christmas loot...perhaps he remembers what the contraption photographed was, because Suzanne does not!

Marc and Christian in their upstairs bedroom on Robertson Academy Road. This is a race car track..

"Nana," Sara Sudekum Stengel and her grandsons from left: Marc, Betsy Stengel Joy and Maurice Joy's first born, Craig Joy, Eric and Christian Stengel

Kermit and Eric around 1965

Family picnic off road on way to the Montreal Expo 1967. Kermit is taking the photo.

Family trip to Montreal with Kermit, Suzanne, Marc, Christian and Eric attending the Montreal Expo 1967. Kermit is taking the photo.

This very famous bull was named FATHER OF THE YEAR at the Montreal Expo in 1967.

Peach Cobbler Stories

Marc dressed for a school play at Christmas time

Marc

May 9, 1981

The artist
The writer, the poet, the filmmaker
The dreamer of idealistic dreams
The student of the world
The inquisitive, analytical, investigative mind
The reserved, somewhat suppressed demeanor
The dignity of bearing, the formality of manner
The fervor, his cause, any cause
Set him aside to another time, another place
The young man was long ago the man

Suzanne

Christian in tournament mode

Christian

May 9, 1981

At twenty-two he is a man
A young man
A strapping blond man with dimples when he smiles
His eyes dance with mischief mostly
Sometimes they are pensive and sad
Always the funny sense of humor is there
The silly names he gives people,
The imaginative expressions which come out of his head,
The deep concern and tenderness he feels for everything
And everyone
His ambition to be a fisherman in Maine
Or a Lawyer
Or a Social Worker
Or a Tennis Teacher
All beautifully packagd in a young man of twenty-two

Suzanne

Eric in his cowboy hat, sitting at a painted school desk Suzanne found in an antique shop

Eric

May 9, 1981

At nineteen he is still a bit of a colt
His thick dark mane carefully groomed
His piercing, deep set black eyes
His boyish grin
His appealing shyness
His manner sometimes sure, at times unsure
His eloquent body language
His bright mind, curious, searching,
learning as he goes
His need for love and affection
His need for the support and reassurance
he has not always had
He feels his way, he stumbles, he learns and
he moves forward
The young colt soon gives way to the young man

Suzanne

Christian's Fourth Birthday & Marc's Seventeenth

I remember planning a party for Christian's fourth birthday. That year, the 28th of March fell once again around Easter time. Christian was born on Holy Saturday in 1959. Chris and I had great fun preparing for his party. We colored eggs, discussed the guest list of his little friends, and planned the food we would have for the children. It was to be a small party of four or five friends. Before the guests were due to arrive, I put out the clothes Christian was going to wear. Of course they were "party clothes" or "Sunday clothes" as was the custom (and I think, still is) among the younger set. Light blue short pants, white shirt, white socks and white shoes. We got everything on, without major objections, but when it came to putting on white shoes and socks, Christian was adamant about not wearing those. I cajoled, then it turned into an argument with this sweet little four year old and in the end, he strongly resolved not to wear the white shoes. It soon became a battle of wills. Looking back, I don't know why I didn't bend at the first sign of objection. I certainly didn't want to upset him, but I unwittingly managed to do just that.

At that point the doorbell rang and the children and their parents began arriving. For the most part the children were dropped off by the parents. So here are four or five playmates and no birthday boy. He wouldn't even come down from his room with shoes or without. Kermit arrived in time for the party, only to find Christian not present at the festivities. He went up to Christian's room and after a very long time, just as the parents were arriving to pick up their children to take them home, Kermit came down carrying

Christian who looked very forlorn. It made me sad. Unfortunately, I was so caught up in the party and the festivities that I had neglected to consider, or even notice how miserable Christian was, wearing the "party clothes," not just the shoes, mind you. He was too embarrassed to be seen in something he wore only on special occasions. These were playmates and he didn't dress that way for play. That was a sad lesson learned by this mother on that day.

It turns out Kermit had an identical reaction to a birthday party given to him by his parents when he was a little boy. Under very similar conditions, he too, had been a "no show" birthday boy just like Christian. I soon learned that in my family of all men, parties were not the way they wished to celebrate special occasions. That was a sad acknowledgement and disappointing to me, for I do love family parties and dinners with good friends. I suppose I am much more of a social animal than any of the men in my family — including my brother Pierre — and of course Kermit and our sons. Such is life...not such a bad thing if everyone gives a little.

I tried my hand (I'm a slow learner and I love parties!) once more when, with the help of Marc's friends, I planned a surprise 17th birthday party for Marc. That was a near disaster because Marc was caught totally off guard and hated every minute of it. I served sparkling white grape juice to everyone and later found out that some of the 16 and 17 year old guests told their parents that Marc had champagne at his party. One of the culprits in that rumor was Will Akers, I believe. I was very surprised to hear it, for I had not taken into account the lack of sophistication among some of our young guests. I think the 16 and 17 year olds had a good time. I don't remember. What I do remember is striking out for the second time. I vowed then and there that there would not be a third strike. Slow, I might be, stupid I am not!

I remember Eric, around age 7, wanting to earn a little money. What he really wanted to do was sell paper hats which he made himself out of newspapers. You know the old triangular ones —

the sea admiral ones. That little rascal managed to sell a few. What a funny and creative little boy he was! I suggested other things and he decided on going around the neighborhood offering to polish anything brass. He equipped himself with a cigar box that contained brass polish and a couple of rags. He charged .25 for a door knob and .50 for andirons. He was a very enterprising young man and much to my surprise came home with a little bit of money, for he had found several willing clients. They loved his industrious nature. I think everyone was a very good sport paying this little guy for his original idea. After all, who can turn away a .25 purchase to encourage a young boy?

Christian's Nightmares

I remember Christian having nightmares for a certain period in his young life. It lasted several months. Not only were there nightmares, he sometimes cried out in his sleep, and he was also given to sleepwalking. After hearing his cries, one time, I ran upstairs only to find him on all fours trying to pick the specs out of the linoleum tile on the floor. That alarmed me. I tried to wake him up. Once he was awake he was fine. However, a pattern seemed to develop and Kermit and I noticed that he would have these nightmares on Sunday nights. I don't know who came up with the name "the weeklies" but these recurring episodes happened only once a week and on Sunday nights.

Gradually, Christian was able to talk about what was bothering him. It had everything to do with having to go back to school the next day. Christian enjoyed his time at home over the weekend with his brothers, his mother and father and it was a wrench for him to anxiously anticipate a school week that would interrupt his feelings of comfort around home on the weekends.

It troubled me because for the longest time, I didn't know the source of these nightmares. He would cry in his sleep and could only be comforted if we woke him up. I remember thinking that I could more easily deal with a broken arm, which we could have repaired, than with an emotional disturbance unclear to any of us at the time. Christian himself, by opening up to us, shed light on his anxiety about leaving the weekends behind as Mondays loomed large on the horizon.

Poor little Christian, how I ached for him during this period. In this day and time, parents would rush their children to the psychiatrist, or a psychologist, but that was not part of our thinking at the time. It did resolve itself in time, but who is to know, outside of Christian himself, how difficult and painful that period was. Not knowing was very painful for me, I do know that.

Eric's Fishing Pole

Another anecdote: I purchased a fishing pole for Eric because he so enjoyed fishing in Richland Creek near our home in Belle Meade. Eric was 8 or 9 years old at the time. He seemed very pleased with the new fishing pole, I thought. A couple of days later, I inquired about the fishing and how did he like the pole, etc. I was in his room and I happened to glance over in the corner and I saw a fishing pole. Not the fishing pole I had purchased, mind you, a nicer one, a more expensive one. When I asked where it had come from, Eric told me it had come from Ace Hardware, the same store where I had purchased the original pole. After a little more questioning, Eric told me he had exchanged it because he liked the one he had gotten much better. I had seen that same pole in the hardware store and I knew it was more expensive, so I asked Eric if he had given the salesman extra money in this exchange. Eric, to his great credit, told me he had not. I explained that this was a dishonest transaction and that we must go back to the store right away and explain to the salesman exactly what had happened.

Eric was shaking in his boots, but he knew he had to make this right. We entered Ace Hardware and I asked to see the store manager. The manager came out of his back office and I told him that Eric had something to tell him. Eric told the story, the whole truth and nothing but. The manager said that he was glad Eric had told him about the fishing pole and that he should never do that again. The manager was willing to let it be an even exchange, but I insisted that we follow the transaction to its rightful conclusion. Eric then paid the difference with his own money, and that was the end of the fishing pole story

One of many honors earned by Marc Stengel

Jumpology: Marc Stengel

Christian Stengel with three other top tennis players in the Boys "A" Division in the Chattanooga Rotary Tournament

CHRIS S. STENGEL, A, appeared on a segment of a week-long television news feature in Nashville celebrating the twenty-fifth anniversary of the Peace Corps. He is serving the Peace Corps in Togo, a former French mandate in West Africa in a small village near Dapango. Stengel, who speaks fluent French, is trying to encourage farmers to increase production by the animal traction system. He said the hardest part of the job is getting people to accept you, adding that conversation generally doesn't get past the topic of weather. Stengel appeared on the WSMV-TV segment with the village fathers and a young black friend who helps him persuade the farmers to change their approach to farming. He also was shown in the tiny isolated house where he lives alone. The day before the television cameras surprised him by moving into the village, he had cut his own straight blonde hair with a Swiss army knife. His father, **Kermit C. Stengel, Jr.,** A'51, a Nashville commercial realtor, reports that WSMV-TV gave him the two-hour taping session when the station learned that Chris was his son.

It was the 25th Anniversay of the Peace Corps, and Christian was videotaped by Mark O'Neill for WSMV-TV while in Togo. Mark O'Neill attends The Cathedral of the Incarnation where Suzanne worships, and she sees Mark and his wife Bobbie O'Neill just about every Sunday. Another one of those "Small World" exclamations. Christian did some important work in Togo. He managed to convince the farmers to change their arduous approach to farming by first teaching the farmers to harness their wild boars to till the soil. They had been tilling the soil by hand for centuries. He might have had some difficulty earning their trust, but in time, they responded to him wholeheartedly. In fact, the villagers signed a petition of sorts, to the Peace Corps officials asking that Christian be allowed to stay in Togo to finish the job they had begun with Chris. As a rule, the Peace Corps commitment is for 24 months. In Chris' case it was extended to 36 months. The entire village came to say goodbye when he left after three years in their midst.

Piere and Anne Shirley Lafond's Children: From left: Denise, Lise Anne, Michelle and Grandmother Léa Lafond

From left: Pierre Lafond, Lise Anne, Grandmother Léa Lafond, barely visable behind the picnic basket Denise, and next to her, David

Top of photo: Michelle, Lise Anne and Grandmother Léa Lafond

The Lafond cousins. Children of Lise Anne and Pierre Lafond: from left: Denise, David, Lise Anne and Michelle Lafond

Eugene Dobbins was a long time friend of Kermit's who worked for the Tony Sudekum family. Kermit made a point of seeing Eugene from time to time. Kermit took Eugene's picture on Christmas Day 1965.

Photo from left: Ann Street, Sandra's sister, Delphine Jones, Suzanne Lafond and Sandra Jones Werthmann at The Palm Bay Club, Miami, FL

Suzanne and Kermit Stengel at The Swan Ball, Nashville, TN. Suzanne's dress was a soft pink color.

Newly employed at WPLN-FM, 90.3 in Nashville in 1976, three weeks after a car accident. The driver who hit her disregarded a stop sign at Tyne and Belle Meade Blvd., and left the scene of the accident.

New job at WPLN after aforementioned accident. By the way, an attorney friend witnessed the accident and told Kermit Stengel, who tracked down the culprit.

Peach Cobbler Stories

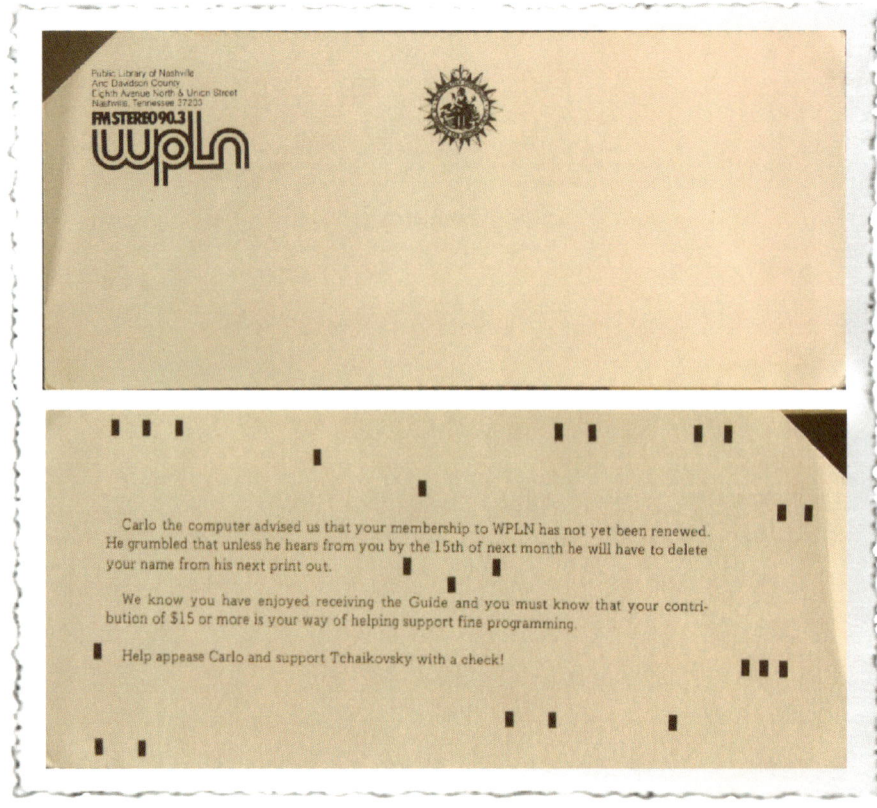

WPLN Promotional piece: Trying to be creative with her fundraising approach at WPLN, Suzanne came up with this mock-up computer card which read "Carlo the computer advised us that your membership to WPLN has not yet been renewed. He grumbled that unless he hears from you by the 15th of next month, he will have to delete your name from his next print out. We know you have enjoyed receiving the Guide and you must know your contribution of $15 or more is your way of helping support fine programming. Help appease Carlo and support Tchaikovsky with a check" -Suzanne Lafond, WPLN 1976-1980

"Action Auction" Fundraiser for PBS Preview Party: Suzanne with artist Danny Aguila

Nashville Symphony Guild announces new officers

Suzanne as chairman of fundraiser with entertainer Danny Davis

*Suzanne with items selected for
PBS's Action Auction at Harpeth Gallery*

Suzanne photographed at the Dessert and Wine Musical Soirée at the Gerald Place home of the Kermit Stengel family. Nashville Symphony musicians entertained.

Kermit and Suzanne were hosting a group of chamber musicians from the Nashville Symphony Orchestra that evening. Photographed standing in the den on Gerald Place, Suzanne is wearing a dark green velvet skirt given to her by her good friend, Ann Street!

Promotion for the Dixie Flyers, who were still the new hockey team in Nashville, having set foot on ice in 1962. A few folks in Nashville knew Suzanne was Canadian, so she was asked to pose with players Ken Murphy on the left, and Ted McCaskill in the center. Suzanne played a little hockey in Montreal at Sacred Heart Convent while in high school. She called it: **Le Hockey.** *Suzanne played goalie! She was told to "Look up" for this photo, which is not so easy while doing a "faceoff."*

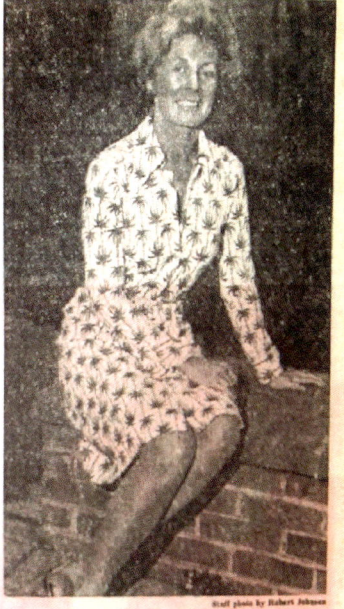

Suzanne photographed as the Action Auction Chairman for The Merry Month of May

Suzanne was the chairman for a fundraiser called "Hello Dolly" to benefit Theater Nashville, as well as the American Cancer Society, with the help of many friends volunteering.

Welcome to Nashville. Suzanne's mother, Léa Moquin Lafond, who has recently moved to Nashville from Montreal, Canada receives a warm welcome. Pictured at the Belle Meade Country Club, left to right are: Suzanne, Mrs. Tony Sudekum, Sara Sudekum Stengel and Léa Moquin Lafond.

The Schooner "Kemal Reis" in the background on the Turkey Coast. Dr. Lee Minton recruited several friends and they chartered this schooner to visit the southern coast of Turkey with a brief stop in Greece. Suzanne remembers the voyage was beautiful and great fun. Lee Minton wearing one of his colorful hats is seen on the left. On the far right is Suzanne. Lee was the only one who knew everyone before the trip. Suzanne recalls they were a very homogeneous group and the mix worked out beautifully.

Van Cliburn in Nashville: Dinner at Dr. Lee Minton's House

Dr. Lee Minton was not only my ophthalmologist, but he was my good friend. He knew I loved to go to the Nashville Symphonic Concerts, and that Kermit was not interested in the least, so I had a standing invitation to join Lee and his friends. All three or four of us left our cars at Peach Blossom Square where Lee lived. As Lee drove, we listened to classical music on WPLN. We tried to come up with the century a particular work was composed while the radio was playing. I knew Chopin and Debussy sometimes, but regarding symphonic composers of the Romantic era, I didn't feel I was in the game. Lee or someone else in our group almost always guessed it right when the announcer identified the music after it had played. It was fun to stab at it and learn as we drove.

Lee was also known for his hospitality when guest soloists came to perform with the Nashville Symphony. He gave beautiful dinner parties. I was invited to be the hostess at many of these dinners. It was always such a nice occasion.

I must mention that Lee had a very special cook, Janie, who prepared dinner for Lee alone, or for Lee's dinner parties. She was a wonderful woman. One special evening, Van Cliburn who had won the International Tchaikovsky competition in Moscow, came to dinner. Lee and Van had become friends after his spectacular win in Russia. It is said that he played Russian music better than the Russians themselves. He was acclaimed the world over. Van Cliburn was an American born in Texas.

After dinner, Janie (whom everyone loved) came into the living room and went directly to Van Cliburn – Janie, untying her apron, asked Van Cliburn if he would play something for her. He said of course and with that Van Cliburn sat at the piano, turned to Janie and asked her what she would like to hear. She said: "Would you play "Amazing Grace?" As he began to play Janie sat next to him on the piano bench and she sang softly the words to "Amazing Grace." There was not a dry eye in the house. It was a beautiful, touching moment I shall never forget.

Today, the radio brought the sad news that Van Cliburn had died in Texas this morning, at age 78, of bone cancer. I felt a rush of memories of dinner with Van Cliburn, of Janie singing "Amazing Grace" accompanied by none other than Van Cliburn the winner of the Tchaikovsky piano competition in 1958! How sweet.

This dinner took place many years after Van Cliburn's memorable win, but Van Cliburn's name will never be forgotten, for he showed the world that a Texas boy could play Tchaikovsky's "Piano Concerto #1," in a way no one else had. Van Cliburn was 23 years old at the time.

I am so glad I was there.

February 27, 2013

The Odeon in Ephesus resembles a small theatre. When the group was there with Dr. Lee Minton, they were told this was the theatre where Saint Paul addressed the Ephesians. Saint Paul came to Ephesus during the time of Emperor Claudius while alterations were still underway at The Theatre.

Ephesus, an ancient city in Greek Asia Minor is in present day western Turkey. It's temple, dedicated to Artemis, was one of the Seven Wonders of the Ancient World. In the Ecumenical Council of 431 AD, it was recorded that when the Virgin Mary came to Ephesus with John,, the patriarch of Antiocheia, who stayed in the house located at the site of the Church of the Virgin Mary, that she was buried in Ephesus.

Portrait painted by Mrs. Houghland for her art class, to which Suzanne was invited to sit as a model.

Very first day on the job as a disc jockey for KKSB, a Santa Barbara radio station, playing Big Band and Jazz music. Suzanne was also selling air time when not doing on-air shifts. Photo taken by a fellow announcer, circa 1986-87.

Time fillers for Suzanne's on-air job as an announcer on KBLS, in Santa Barbara. This was her first job as a DJ.

Kristina Wayborn and Suzanne met at the Los Angeles Broadcasting School. Kristina is a Swedish actress and even though she had been in several movies in Hollywood, she worried that she still had a tinge of her Swedish accent left. She wanted to lose it and thought the broadcasting lessons would help. There was a tiny bit of Swedish accent left, but Suzanne personally thought it added to her charm. Kristina was in the 13th James Bond movie called Octopussy, released in 1983. Kristina and Suzanne became good friends. They would often walk in the park and talk about whatever was on their respective minds. Suzanne spent a couple of

nights at Kristina's apartment after she left Los Angeles and returned to Santa Barbara. Kristina was a very good tennis player and she was invited to play in a celebrity/pro tennis tournament near LA. The two women decided that Suzanne would play the role of her mother at the tournament, just for the fun of it. Many young studs attempted to approach Kristina through Suzanne. One man asked Suzanne how she could have had this long-legged beauty as her child. Kristina was close to six feet in height. Without skipping a beat, Suzanne told the youmg man that Kristina's father was 6'5" and fortunately for Kristina that was where she got her height.. That worked, but at the time Kristina was playing (beautifully, it should be noted) her match and she looked like someone straight out of the movies! She and her various tennis partners won several close matches. After Suzanne returned to Nashville in 1988, she lost track of Kristina. Suzanne believes that she married, but Suzanne doesn't know to whom. She thinks Kristina still lives in California, but isn't sure where. Suzanne thinks of her often and would love to see her again. Someday Suzanne will try to reconnect. She fondly remembers all of her friends of yesteryear.

Carol King from Santa Barbara and Suzanne hiking snowy trails in Yosemite, circa 1981-82

While Suzanne worked for Pierre Lafond at the Santa Barbara Winery, she organized the first ever "Fête des Vandange" – Harvest Street Festival to benefit the Santa Barbara Arts Council. There wasn't a huge turnout with this being the first time, but great fun for all who were there. There was dancing, music, mime, singing and, of course, food and wine. There were souvenir glasses for the first 300 attendees. The gate fee was $5.00 and children were admitted free of charge.

Promotional pamphlet for Santa Barbara YMCA, showing Suzanne loving those aerobic classes!

Petite Fashion Show at one of the Robinson Stores in California. Suzanne Lafond is pictured with actress Debbie Reynolds at the microphone doing commentaries for the show.

Fashion show for Robinson's stores in LA. "Petite Portfolio" actress Debbie Reynolds was the master of ceremony. Suzanne is pictured second from the left.

Suzanne and Pierre at the Santa Barbara airport. Suzanne was flying back to Nashville after a visit with her brother, family and friends.

Pierre Lafond pictured in front of wine cask, testing fermentation at one of his wineries, either Santa Barbara Winery or Lafond Winery and Vineyards

Pierre Lafond, Suzanne's big brother (meaning "older"), has been a wine making pioneer in California's central region. The Lafond vineyards in Santa Ynez began to draw attention worldwide to the region's near perfect weather conditions for the vines.

November 14, 1982

My dear Marc,

Not because I think the writing is good, certainly the form is not, but because the heart dictates randomly, the enclosed thoughts I share with you. It isn't important what prompted each one, in time I scarcely remember myself, but that they find their way to the blank page is what I find to be good. Because, in the past, you encouraged me to do so, I send a few along to you.

Perhaps it is nothing more than a form of therapy. Heaven knows we all need a little from time to time, but this that I call writing, is of great value for me. Not in a literary sense to be sure, but in its very expression.

I miss you, our long talks, our discussions, our secret confidences. I miss your bright mind, your handsome, intelligent face, I miss watching the unique way in which you move and speak. It is very difficult for me to be separated from you and Chris. I miss Dad as well, strange as that may seem. My intention is not to alarm you certainly, because I am getting along very well indeed, but there are times when I am overwhelmed with an intangible sadness which does not last and which I approach quite philosophically so there is no cause for concern, at all. I am ever so grateful to have Eric around. He is a wonderful companion and we share so much of our days together in thought or in deed. We have some hilarious times together and serious ones as well.

You can well imagine how often our conversation turns to you, Chris and to Dad. Dropshot hasn't been mentioned much since he went to live with a new family, and for me it is better left alone.

I think about you daily and I wonder about your lovely friend Terry. I do hope les affaires du coeur are as happy as they can be. I look forward to meeting Terry and I am still shooting for January or February when I shall return to Nashville for a brief stay.

It is late, so I will close. I've had you on my mind so I wanted to drop by and say hello!

Je t'aime,

On a visit to Switzerland while Christian Stengel was studying at the University of Lausanne, Suzanne and son spent a day hiking in the Alps. Circa 1981 or 1982.

Dear Mom

Letter From Christian

What a complex mixture of emotions I'm feeling right now. First of all I'm undeniably sad about us having to part, I, who am so easily able to leave people I care about to head off for a new adventure, realize that leaving my mother will always be painful. I love you so much that you will always reach the innermost part of me. I also feel proud – proud of who you are, what you are doing with your life, and the ideals you stand for. You are an inspiration to me. I feel lucky, too, simply because I am your son and can claim you as my mother – something that only two other people in this world can claim.

These two weeks with you have been a joy for me. I really want you to know that, because in spite of my moodiness and my teasing you, both of which I hope you didn't misinterpret. I enjoy being with you immensely. You are such an important part of my life and always will be.

So know, dear mother, that I consider our relationship a very special one - one that I will always cherish, and one whose growth I will always foster.

I wish you nothing but success, health, and happiness and look with great anticipation to our next meeting (perhaps in Montreal).

All my love,
Chris
July 1985

*Eric Stengel, while studying at
Parsons The New School for Design, NYC.
Photos taken by classmate.*

Eric Stengel in NYC photo shoot

September 1, 1990
Letter to Eric's Wife

Dear Claudia,

I am accustomed to him grown
He is, afterall, twenty-nine and about to be married
But, in my heart of hearts he is still the little dark eyed boy
So dear, such a funny mischievous, unique little boy
Just as you see him in this photograph
Bathed, combed and powdered
Ready for a story on his father's lap
Or a song at his mother's breast
At day's end before sleep that would bring him
The most unbelievable dreams
Products of an active mind and body and a fanciful imagination
It wasn't so long ago...
Today, he is strong, decided, talented, hardworking
Pleased with the appreciation and recognition that eluded him in his early youth
Eager to make his mark, leave his imprint through
Architecture, his designs, his decisions
Many have yet to appreciate the dedication, the drive,
The difficult tasks he has mastered along his
Successful college education
This is his mantle, the weight could be crushing if he did not
Delight in his chosen profession and did not have by his side
The love, support and understanding of his wife and friend, Claudia

With love,
Suzanne

Life After The Divorce

After my divorce, I moved to Santa Barbara, California, after 27 years of marriage to Kermit C. Stengel, Jr.

My first job was at a local bank, the Bank of Montecito.

I was hired as an outside-the-bank banker! In other words, my job was recruiting businesses for the Bank of Montecito. The bank president told me that I didn't need a background in banking to be successful in the job. He said the world is full of people who know everything there is to know about banking. What they needed were my selling and recruiting skills. He told me to let his people take care of the banking and concentrate on doing what I do best. I went to all manner of businesses, from restaurants, to men's clothing stores, to gift shops to retirement communities, singing the praises of the Bank of Montecito.

One day I saw an article in the Santa Barbara newspaper reporting a robbery on Stearns Wharf where a shop owner was attacked on his way to his car. The Wharf was a popular shopping area for restaurants, boutiques and specialty shops, with parking spots at a premium. Most merchants parked near the wharf, but not on it, leaving those premium spaces for customers and tourists. This shop owner I read about, was carrying the day's cash receipts in his briefcase to make a late deposit at his bank, when he was robbed.

This story bothered and preoccupied me. I was upset at the idea that shop owners were in danger, on a daily basis, while they were trying to run their businesses.

I came up with the idea that a courier service was needed to protect the merchants by safely picking up their daily cash receipts and taking them to the bank.

I presented my idea to the bank president who discussed it with other bank officers and they endorsed the concept, saying: "Why didn't we think of that?"

I reminded them that was why they hired me. To think outside the box – the bank in this case.

I took my idea back to the merchants on the wharf and told them that if they would give their commercial accounts to the Bank of Montecito, the bank would provide safe and dependable courier service for their daily cash receipts.

This idea became a reality, providing a win-win for the clients and the bank. First there was a Brinks-type courier service, later a concrete safety deposit structure.

Soon after this development, the bank hired a recent female graduate of Harvard Business School, setting her up in a large office.

I didn't have an office, but I had a desk on the mezzanine with several of my co-workers.

I really didn't need an office just so I had a desk and a telephone. I was after all, an outside the bank business account recruiter.

Shortly after the new hire began working for the bank, she came to my work area and asked me to come with her to her newly occupied office. She asked me to explain exactly what my duties were at the bank. I proceeded to tell her everything I did recruiting commercial accounts for the Bank of Montecito. Making a case for the bank I was representing, to the person to whom I was speaking. I told Ms. Harvard Businees School that I never presented myself as a banker. She asked me if I knew what a 'repo' was. I politely told her that I had been informed that if anybody ever asked me a bank-related question, I would take contact information and let one of the bankers, whose department covered that particular question, get in touch with him or her. It was very straightforward. I told her that there were several very sharp guys in the bank who covered the financial questions and I wasn't trying to do their jobs.

A few days after that initial interview, Ms. Harvard Business School noticed me walking around and talking to several of the bankers in the building, concerning various questions my commercial customers had asked me in my recruiting calls. She walked over to me, complimented me on my suit, and asked where I had purchased the pink tweed suit. I thanked her for the compliment, gave her the name of the store where I had bought the suit. The very next day she walked in wearing the very same suit I owned and had worn the day before.

Talk about someone bulldozing her way through life! Everybody in the bank snickered at her behind her back, with a wink in my direction.

We developed a strange love-hate working relationship after that. I didn't know her enough to actually hate her, I just didn't particularly like her.

Two or three weeks go by. She calls me down to her office again. I was wondering if maybe she needed a personal shopper or what exactly was on her mind. When I arrived at her office, she informed me without preamble, reason or explanation that I was fired. I was forbidden to finish up any impending deals, or to contact anyone. I thought she was kidding. She wasn't. She told me to get my briefcase and purse, and to leave immediately.

My head was reeling. I couldn't believe my ears. I wasn't even allowed to go back to my desk. However, I did ask one of my co-workers to go to my area and retrieve some business folders that belonged to me, not the bank. She said she would and she did. I retrieved the folders from her at a later date.

Santa Barbara condo purchased in 1982, located at 1221-A Salsipuedes N.

*Suzanne's 50th birthday portrait,
taken by Marc Stengel in Santa Barbara*

*Julia Child and Suzanne Lafond working on guest list for the coming week for the **Dinner at Julia's** TV series.
Photo by Paul Child*

Julia, Paul and Me

After the debacle at the Bank of Montecito, and the abrupt end of my job at the bank, in time I cooled my heels over this unexpected turn of events, and called my brother, Pierre, who had various businesses in town. My brother is a man of few words, but you always know where his heart is. He never blinks or makes excuses. If family is concerned, he immediately takes action.

He promptly offered me a job as a wine rep for his wines. I took some courses with the staff, learned as much as possible as fast as I could, and Pierre turned me loose. I made some calls locally and in Los Angeles.

One evening after a brief time of working for Pierre, I received a phone call from a person who sounded very much like the famed chef, Julia Child. I assumed it was a friend, making a prank call as a joke. Everyone knew Paul and Julia Child owned a condo near the beach, in Santa Barbara. I listened to the voice and reflected a moment and decided that it was indeed Julia Child calling.

She had been given my name by a mutual friend as a possible publicist for an upcoming 13-episodes of a show called *Dinner at Julia's*. She and her husband, Paul, wanted to interview me. Julia informed me that two or three other candidates were under consideration.

She was calling on a Saturday, asking if I was available for a meeting the following Monday at 6:00 PM.

I had to inform her that at 6:00 PM on Mondays, Wednesdays and Fridays I was committed to taking aerobic exercise classes at the YMCA, so I wasn't available at that time.

I told her that I'd be glad to meet with her on Tuesday or Thursdays, or even the weekend.

There was a slight pause on the end of the phone line. I don't think Julia Child was accustomed to having people put her on hold.

Now you might wonder why I didn't just change my schedule to fit hers, but there was a method to my madness. I wanted her to know that I was committed to my exercise regimen or to whatever else I was doing and it was important to me to honor my commitments, whatever they were.

I did meet with Julia on Tuesday at 6:00 PM at their condo. Julia and Paul had a glass of wine, but I chose instead to have a glass of orange juice.

Julia described the job, telling me that the main publicity duties would be performed by her long time publicity group in New York. My job would be to work with her and other staff members as her California liaison with New York.

I soon became the Santa Barbara go-to-girl on the set of *Dinner at Julia's.*

The following Saturday, Bob, her attorney from Boston, was in town to interview the prescreened candidates.

The four of us each had our moment with Bob, stating our cases.

Bob didn't give any of us a definitive answer at the meeting. He left things very open-ended, until he discussed his impressions with Julia.

So I left the meeting thinking it had gone well, but without a job offer in hand.

Later that same Saturday, Bob called me to say that he was leaving Sunday morning, and invited me to have breakfast with him before his flight for Boston.

This was very good news to me. I considered this to be a "callback," as in auditions which were very familiar to me. At this point, I felt I had a real chance at landing the job. Just another hurdle, but things looked good to me.

The breakfast was very pleasant and conversational, and he told me that he would call me back Monday night with an answer.

Monday night the phone rang, and I was offered the position.

I immediately went to work with the rest of the crew, taping episodes at Fess Parker's Ranch, the estate of the star of the classic movie *Davy Crockett* and the long-running television series, *Daniel Boone*.

The production team was headed by Russell Morash, who had worked with Julia in Boston at WGBH from the very beginning of Julia's career in cooking shows on TV. Julia, Russell, and his wife Miriam were a team as well as others from WGBH who had also worked with Julia over the years.

The kitchen, a den-like room where cocktails were served before the show and the dining room were the main areas used in the rented house, and of course, the kitchen, lest we forget!

Working with Julia was truly a dream job for me. My main duty was to invite food editors from the nation's major newspapers to come as guests to Santa Barbara and join other guests for cocktails. The dinner itself was more structured. Julia invited a guest chef to every taping. A guest winemaker, special friends of hers and Paul's and other luminaries in the food and wine world. There were ten guests at the table with Julia at the head of table and Paul at the foot of the table for all the dinner tapings of *Dinner at Julia's*.

It was a delightful assignment to be working with Julia and her crew. It is safe to say that Julia was universally loved and getting guests to join her for dinner was the easiest task I've ever had!

Most of the food editors were already dedicated to her and her pioneering efforts, so it was more like a homecoming with special friends than a work assignment for all the food writers around the country. She knew them all at this point.

I came to know Julia and Paul very well. I soon observed that the people who came to the cocktail parties and the dinners immediately gravitated towards Julia. She had true star power, and more often than not, Paul was ignored by the fawning crowds. He was ten years older than Julia, and had begun to fade in health by this time, with early onset of dementia. He was a dear, dear soul, and I became devoted to him. Julia had the attention of the entire production team, the visiting guests, and the public at large, so she didn't need my personal attention at the gatherings that were being taped. Paul, on the other hand, was often left alone on the sidelines. Often seen with his camera, Paul took his own set of photos. He was a fine photographer.

Whereas Julia was very outgoing, Paul was quiet and reserved. Julia told me once that she was born a ham, and she meant it. I silently agreed with that assessment. Maybe that's why they made such a good couple. They complemented one another.

Paul was very talented. He was a Renaissance man, in my view. His paintings, photography and drawings were artistically beautiful. His sketches were featured in the early cookbooks. They were pen and ink drawings demonstrating how a bird, turkey or hen should be carved, among other pen and ink drawings.

Julia was unique in every way: her distinctive voice, her outgoing personality, even her physical being. Julia was six feet, two and a half inches tall, and one of my duties was to order the yellow fisherman slicker outfit she wore when we took the television production team on location to Seattle, Washington for a segment on salmon fishing. It was difficult finding one that would fit her. Forget finding one in a woman's size for her frame. I was lucky to locate a man's size that worked just fine. She was bigger than life in many ways.

My office was a small room near the kitchen, and one day I overheard some discussion between Julia and Russell, the show's director. It wasn't an argument, but I felt they were having an ardent discussion. Julia was trying to get away part of the afternoon and Russ, the producer, was very insistent that the taping had to be done that day, and couldn't be delayed for obvious scheduling concerns. It was apparent that tensions were on the rise.

I quietly ventured into the kitchen, looked at Julia, and said: "Julia, is there something I can do to help?"

Julia turned around, looked at me and exclaimed how thankful she was that I came to offer my help. Mind you I had no idea what the fuss was all about, but on the chance that I could be of help, I wanted to offer. She asked me if I would mind taking Paul to a 2:00 pm eye-doctor appointment that afternoon. Normally, Julia would have been the one to take Paul to the doctor, of course, but with the entire crew in need of Julia to complete the shooting schedule for the day, leaving the set would have put the shooting behind schedule.

I was very happy I could be of help.

Julia asked me to accompany Paul to the appointment and to take detailed notes as to the doctor's instructions, since Paul often couldn't remember details.

The appointment was met, notes were duly taken, and all was well.

Proving that I could handle these newly added duties, I was soon trusted with this responsibility on a regular basis, freeing Julia to concentrate on her television show safe in the knowledge that Paul's medical needs were being given proper attention.

This pleased me because I had deep regard for Julia and Paul.

We enjoyed each other's company.

Even on weekends when we weren't working on the television show, Julia would call me and invite me to join them for hamburgers in Carpenteria. It was one of Julia's and Paul's favorite spots on the weekend. I would always offer to pick them up, and I did. We enjoyed a fun meal together outside the work environment.

At the time, I had a Mercedes 300D automobile which was nice and comfortable, and Julia liked riding with me as it gave her a break from the usual driving during weekends.

Our lives were intertwined in a delicious way on and off the set!

On many Fridays after the week's shooting, Julia liked to take many of us to dinner. Not for the camera, but to enjoy a relaxed evening together. Russell and Marian, local friends and a food writer, perhaps. Those of us who were not part of the *Dinner at Julia's* TV table.

Julia and I would get together on Monday mornings and discuss the guests list for the Friday dinners. We got in the habit of going to the El Encanto Hotel in the foothills overlooking Santa Barbara. Not only a splendid setting, but excellent food that Julia could count on.

I was always invited to those dinners. Julia and Paul made me feel very welcome as a full member of the group.

Julia would be seated at the head of the table, as always, Paul was at the other end, and the guests filling up the chairs between Paul and Julia.

I sat immediately to Paul's right, so I could pay attention to him while all eyes were on Julia at the other end.

At one of these dinners, I was talking to Paul at our quiet end of the table while others were looking in Julia's direction and chatting as one does at dinner. My left hand was on the table just a bit of my forearm and we were quietly talking when Paul put his right hand over mine, and patted my hand, saying "Suzanne, I'm going to tell you something that I want you to take in the very best possible way." I smiled at him, and said "Paul, what is it?" I asked.

"I love you," Paul said.

With that, I took my hand from under his hand, and I covered his hand with my left hand, and told him that I wanted him to take what I was going to say in the very best possible way, I then told Paul I loved him too. I have to say it was a sweet moment all around…and we both meant it.

We were worlds apart but we did love one another in a sweet and caring way. I will not soon forget his heartfelt words. Paul was a prince of a guy.

Paul lost his twin brother during the taping of the *Dinner at Julia's* series. When I heard about the death, I wrote Paul a note of condolence, which he carried inside his jacket's breast pocket. It touched me that he cared enough to carry it with him. He pulled it out of his breast pocket to show me he had it with him. It was a lovely, unexpected friendship we shared during these many weeks of production of the *Dinner at Julia's* show.

There was a large rock on the grounds of Fess Parker's house. It sloped toward the Pacific Ocean. Paul could often be found there quietly meditating. When possible, I would join him there just to talk.

We worked on the show from February until June 1983. We had the wrap party at Fess Parker's ranch, in the large kitchen where a lunch bar with stools could accommodate most of us or around a near breakfast table. I found myself seated next to Bob Vila, the man who starred on the acclaimed PBS television series, *This Old House*. He was very curious as to how a French-Canadian girl came to live in Nashville, Tennessee and then wound up in Santa Barbara, California working with Julia Child on a television series.

I explained that my brother had been in Santa Barbara since 1956 and that I had come to Santa Barbara from Nashville in 1981 after a divorce. Bob asked me if I ever thought about going back to Nashville. I told him that I was thinking about going back because when I left Nashville, my three sons were scattered to the winds, I was going through a divorce, and there was nothing keeping me in Nashville. I told Bob that I had some reservations about going back.

I had recently called my former mother-in-law, Kermit's mother, (Sara Sudekum Stengel), to wish her a happy birthday, casually mentioning that I was thinking about moving back to Nashville. She said: "I wouldn't do that!" in a cautionary tone. Her reaction surprised me, and I asked her why shouldn't I go back? She said all I would do is cause trouble! I asked her to tell me if I had ever caused trouble for my family? I had left Nashville very quietly during the divorce proceedings. She couldn't give me an answer, so the conversation was ended.

Bob Vila looked at me eye to eye and said: "Where is your heart?"

I replied that my heart was with my children. He said, then "go back." It was probably the nudge I needed from a third party with no vested interest.

Julia Child and Suzanne Lafond checking the guest list for **Dinner at Julia's** *TV series. Photo by Paul Child*

Paul and Julia Child, when renovations of the kitchen were taking place in Fess Parker's home, which was rented for the TV series

Peach Cobbler Stories

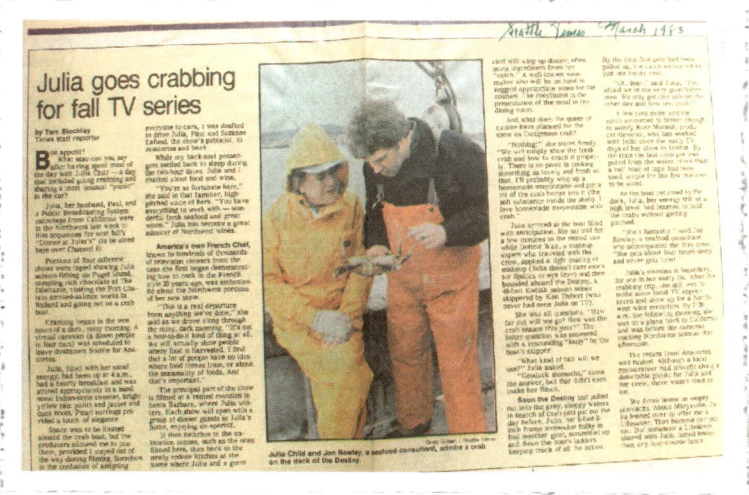

Julia on location for a crab course for her TV show

Julia in date country for TV show

A party for Paul Child highlighted by the **Los Angeles Times**

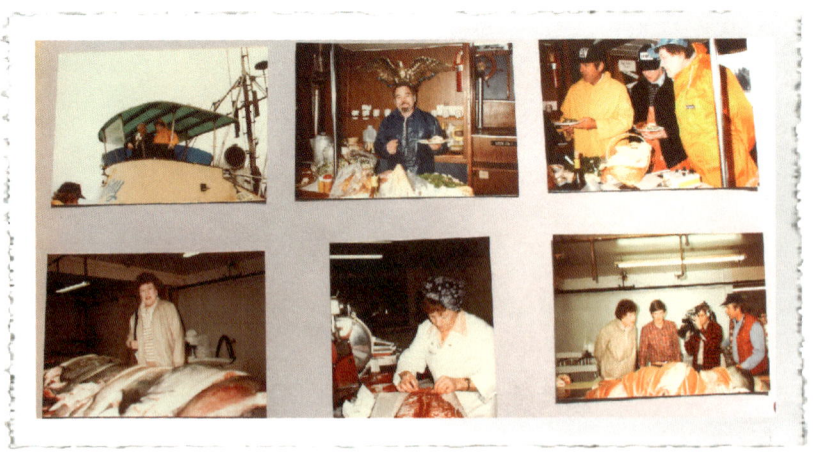

Julia Child on location for the filming of **Dinner at Julia's** *TV series where each dinner course was discussed*

Suzanne Lafond, Paul and Julia Child in Santa Barbara

Suzanne Lafond, Julia Child and staffer wear souvenir tee-shirts.

*An exhibition of Paul Child's paintings,
pen & ink drawings and his photography*

*Press kit for **Dinner at Julia's** TV series*

Santa Ynez Valley

A quiet moment for Julia and Paul Child while overlooking Santa Barbara harbor

*Julia Child in Fess Parker's home, where the kitchen was remodeled for **Dinner at Julia's** TV series*

*Julia salmon fishing in Seattle for **Dinner at Julia's**, her new TV series*

Julia puts on a barbecue for her TV series, Suzanne with a guest chef.

Peach Cobbler Stories

Julia on a shrimp boat in her search for the freshest ingredients for her TV series

Julia and her wonderful crew from WGBH Boston taping footage for **Dinner at Julia's**

Julia Child picking artichokes for
Dinner at Julia's *in Salinas, CA*

Peach Cobbler Stories

Julia Child and crew in Santa Barbara harbor finding crabs for dinner on location for **Dinner at Julia's** *TV series*

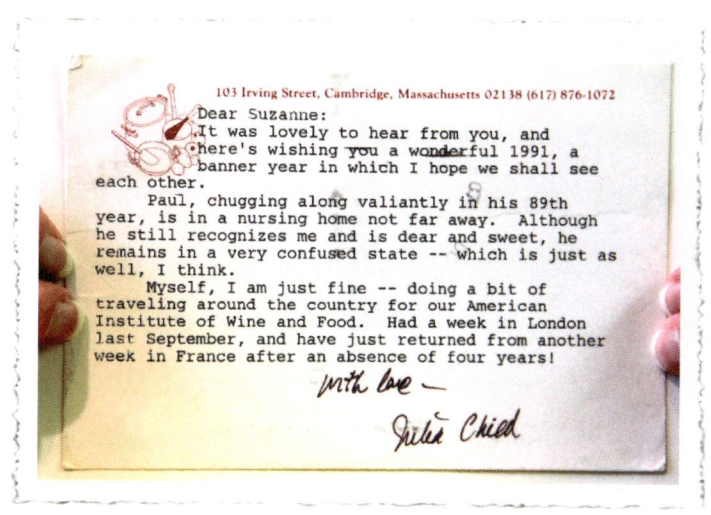

Personal post card to Suzanne from Julia Child

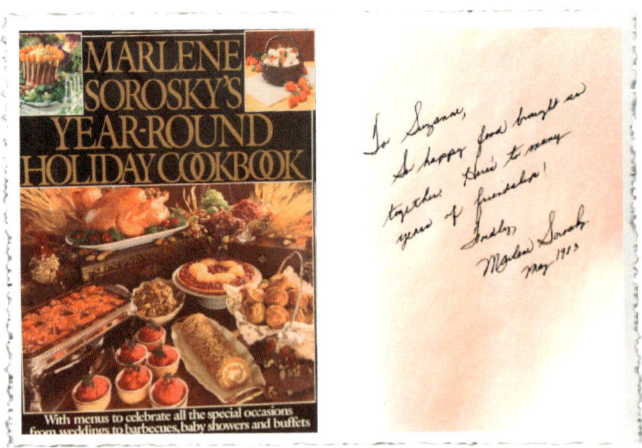

*Marlene Sorosky's **Year-Round Holiday Cookbook**, signed for Suzanne. Marlene continues to make her mark with many beautiful cookbooks. Suzanne met Marlene on the set of the **Dinner at Julia's** TV series in 1983. Their friendship developed easily and naturally from that point.*

*The **Dessert Lover's Cookbook** is another beautiful book by Marlene Sorosky, one of several that Suzanne owns. She considers the book a must have in any dessert lover's cookbook library.*

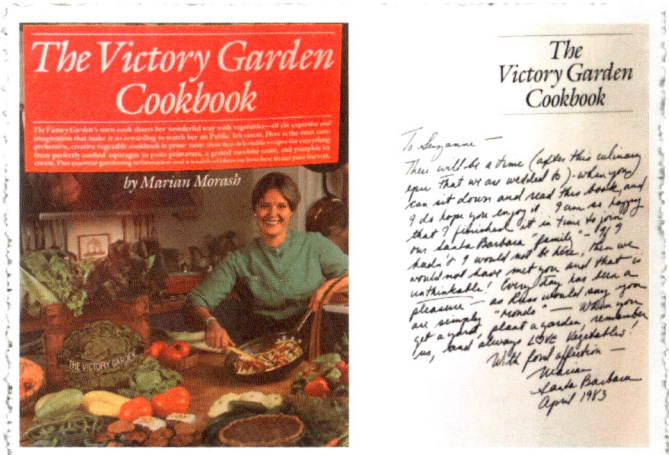

The Victory Garden Cookbook by Marian Morash is one of Suzanne's treasured books. Marian is a "Vedette" in her own right. She is the wife of Russell Morash, who was Julia Child's producer for her entire television career. Marian and Russell Morash welcomed Suzanne warmly and graciously into the **Dinner at Julia's** television family. Suzanne has enjoyed Marian's **Victory Garden Cookbook since** 1983.

*Upstairs at Pierre Lafond's store with Marian Morash signing her **Victory Garden Cookbook**. Wendy Foster is talking to her in the photograph.*

*Cookbook author, Marian Morash, signing her **Victory Garden Cookbook**, upstairs at Pierre Lafond's store in Santa Barbara*

Peach Cobbler Stories

Suzanne on the right with the Los Angeles 1984 Olympic Mascot. Photo taken in Los Angeles.

Suzanne at Lake Casitas in front of the crowd watching the regatta competitions.

The Los Angeles Olympics

The summer of 1984 brought the Olympics to Los Angeles, and I wanted to be a part of that. I volunteered to be an interpreter for the two official languages of the games: French and English. Normally the third language would be that of the host country, but in this case that was already covered by English, albeit with an American accent.

I was trained in Los Angeles by the organizing committee LAOOC, and was assigned to the Regatta venue: kayaking, canoeing and rowing at Lake Casitas, a beautiful lake about 40 minutes from Santa Barbara. I was involved in recruiting and training, having started the job at the Pre-Olympic trials in 1983, right after my job with Julia Child came to an end with the completion of the television series.

I enjoyed that job immensely. I trained the other interpreters and all I had to know was English and French even if the interpreters were Polish or German, Chinese or Japanese or any of the other languages of the world.

We had "walkie-talkies" (the dark ages by today's technology advances) to keep in touch with each other. One day during the Pre-Olympic trials I had a call from a doctor in the infirmary saying he needed someone immediately. I arrived to find three doctors talking together, discussing a young athlete from the Ivory Coast. The athlete was asking for something and nobody could figure out what he needed. I went to the gurney, where the man was lying and saw this 17-year old male. I asked him in French what he needed, and he told me that he wanted "that medicine that makes you strong." I immediately knew that he was asking for illegal steroids.

He said that he wanted to "be a big man."

I asked him if his father was "a big man." He said yes. I asked if his father had brothers, and were they also big men? Yes, he replied, that his uncles were also big. I looked at him and told him that he was still growing, that his body was developing and getting stronger every day, and soon he would be a big man himself. I told him that he didn't need the steroids he was asking for, that they were illegal and very dangerous to his health, in fact those drugs could kill him. I told him to believe that he would grow into a big man without drugs, if he would just let nature take its course. He smiled at me.

Meanwhile the doctors were standing around waiting to hear what transpired between the young athlete and me. When I told them that I had talked him out of requesting steroids, everyone seemed very relieved.

That moment was a sensitive encounter that has stayed with me over the years as one of those fond memories of the Olympics. Whenever our paths would cross around Lake Cassitas, the young athlete smiled and waved at me. I was grateful to see a smile on his face!

During the 1983 pre-Olympic trials I was returning to Santa Barbara from Los Angeles for a teaching session with new recruits: Korean, Vietnamese, Polish, German, Italian, Spanish, Norwegians and Swedes were some of the nationalities represented. No, of course I don't speak all those languages. Remember what I wrote about the official languages used in Olympic competitions. Since we were the host country, French and English were the only two official languages for volunteers and staff. All the interpreters of the various languages spoke English, plus their native languages. We were extremely well covered.

Some instructional videos were to arrive in time for an afternoon workshop in interpreting at Lake Casitas. The videos were to help me in the workshop I would be conducting that day. I finally received a message after the class had begun that the videos did not make it. I was told to ad-lib whatever I had learned in Los Angeles. I managed very well, considering.

One of the key elements in interpreting is you do not call attention to yourself, and you interpret using the first pronoun throughout. In other words, you become the person for whom you are interpreting.

To make it more fun, I added some of the things an interpreter must never do: chew gum, scratch one's self, play with any part of one's clothing or hair, or clean one's eyeglasses. You get the picture. The verboten elements lent themselves readily to some pretty silly demonstrations, I assure you. My silly self was in full gear!

Because I am an early riser, I drove from Santa Barbara to Lake Casitas early, arriving before 5:00 AM each day. It gave me time to check with the National Weather Service, and I wrote the weather prediction for each day on what was then an early version of today's computer. The wind speed was very important, for rowing, kayaking and perhaps more so, for the canoeing competition. We began the races early before the wind speed would rise. Each team captain would check the weather report I had posted in the main trailer where they went after arriving at the lake. What a beautiful sight it was to see rowboats, canoes and kayaks glide across Lake Casitas in near perfect weather – most days. I will not soon forget that beautiful sight.

The class of recruits for the languages department turned out to be highly dependable and professional during the Olympics, except for one lady from Columbia, South America who didn't seem to understand the uniform requirements. While all the rest of us wore uniform laced-up Oxford-style shoes, she insisted on wearing high heels, which were totally inappropriate for covering the rugged terrain at the venue. Part of interpreting work consisted of going to the various publicity tents for speeches and interviews, as well as to the various teams' headquarters when needed. All that meant hiking over sometimes rough terrain and getting there as quickly as summoned.

Since it wasn't my job to be the chief enforcer of the uniform code, I just let her continue with her silly shoes and watched her wobble and teeter-totter her way through the Olympics. Eventually one of the commissioners noticed the big effort to get her from here to there and took it upon himself to put her into the uniform shoes she should have been wearing from the beginning.

Peter Ueberroth, who was the Director of the Los Angeles Olympic Organizing Committee (LAOOC) in 1984, visited Lake Casitas one day and asked the Commissioner at Lake Casitas who I was. He was told, then he passed on a compliment to the Commissioner that our language services department was the best he had seen at any of the venues for those 1984 Games. O.K.!

Since I was the director at our facility, I took that as a very high compliment. We were very organized and the interpreters took their responsibilities seriously. It was wonderful to be appreciated for our efforts. Perfection isn't what we achieved. However, lots can be said for a band of strangers pulling their oars in unison.

Peter Ueberroth did a splendid job, running the Games at a profit for the first time in many, many years. So many other host cities had previously gone deeply in the red with their games, leaving huge debts for taxpayers to pick up when the crowds and media had gone home. That wasn't the case with the 1984 Olympics.

Lake Casitas in California, site of the 1984 Olympic Regatta where canoeing, rowing, and kayaking competitions took place.

Pre-Olympic gathering shown with the German Commissioner flanked by interpreters and Suzanne Lafond, Director of Language Services for the Regatta event at Lake Casitas, CA

Côte d'Ivoire athletes participating in the Olympic Regatta with Suzanne Lafond, French/English interpreter, and with official volunteer in foreground on the right.

*Vintage dresses fashion show to benefit charity.
Suzanne is the third woman from left of photo –
the only white-haired woman there!*

*Suzanne, Jane Entrekin and Ann Bernard attending yet
another fundraiser, this one at Cheekwood*

Back in Nashville

The fall of 1984, I came for a visit to Nashville. I stayed with my son Marc and his lovely wife Terry, who had started their own family.

My ex-husband suggested that I consider moving into Arden Place, near David Lipscomb College in the Green Hills area of Nashville. I had watched the development going up in the 1970s, and was very familiar with the property. I would pass it on the way to bringing the children from school each day.

I looked at other places, but always came back to Arden Place.

I returned to Nashville after an absence of not quite eight years spent in Santa Barbara and Los Angeles. The year was 1988.

My three sons, Marc, Christian and Eric were no longer living at home when I moved to California.

Marc and Terry had two daughters while I was on the West Coast. I was not in Nashville at their births, and it tore my heart up being so far away from my family at such milestone moments. Their first daughter is Mary Elizabeth Stengel, and their second daughter is Morgan Elen Stengel.

I was so eager to be with my grandchildren, that was the reason for my decision to move back to Nashville.

I told Marc that I didn't come back to Nashville to baby sit, though I would in any emergency.

I made a deal with Marc and Terry that, if they allowed, I would pick up Mary and Morgan every Saturday, around 10:00 AM and take them to Davis-Kidd bookstore in Green Hills to listen to the story hour. Then we would have lunch together, and everybody seemed happy with that arrangement. I certainly was.

They called me *Mamie* which is a contraction of two French words *Mon Amie*, meaning "my friend." It is an endearing term that French children often call their grandmothers. It is also a name that a gentleman who is engaged might call his girlfriend. It is a lovely name in the French language.

My mother was called Mamie by my three sons, and I was glad that we carried on the family tradition.

We would enjoy story time together, and then look at various books on display, before heading to lunch. When they were very young, I'd bring them back to my home in Arden Place and prepare hard-boiled egg salad sandwiches. I would sneak tiny bits of carrots into the salad, along with bits of *cornichons*, which were small midget sweet pickles. I had whole wheat bread or nine-grain bread, which they enjoyed. Then they would usually take a nap, and I was likely to retreat to my bedroom for quiet time. When they woke up, we would either take a walk around Arden Place, which was safe if we were walking, or go to the park. We had many wonderful and different outings together.

I was told by Terry, their mother, that the family would soon be joined by another baby. I asked if it was alright for me to mention it to the girls, and was told that they already knew the BIG news and they were happy about it.

So at our next Saturday outing, I mentioned the news to Mary, who was four years old at the time, while we were eating lunch at the table.

Instead of receiving the news with joy, little Mary started crying her eyes out, and I was overcome with confused emotions. I asked her why she was so upset and she told me that her mother wouldn't love her anymore when the new baby arrived. I told her that her mother would always love her and Morgan and the new baby. Mothers and Fathers love their children, no matter how many there are.

It tore my heart out to see this precious little girl feeling so dejected and rejected at the time. While I know it is not an unusual reaction, I had never experienced it first hand.

Little Sara came and she was a beautiful small angel. She was adorable just like her two sisters. All three of the girls were lovely to look at and wonderful to be with. That is as objective as I can be. They were and remain the loves of my life!

I had many treasured moments with my grandchildren, nourishing my maternal needs and instincts.

We went to craft fairs together at Centennial Park, art galleries occasionally, The Adventure Science Museum, visiting the live bunnies at McClures Department store. Many such activities to share on our Saturdays. We even played hide-and-seek on the property at Arden Place, going to the grassy areas where the big trees are. I would be "it" and the girls would scamper away to hide behind tree trunks. I would pretend to look everywhere but where they were actually hidden, looking under benches, behind bushes, ignoring the obvious spots. They weren't so hard to find because often I would hear giggles from their hiding places. I acted like I'd heard not a peep!

We had such fun together.

Around 3:00 or 4:00 in the afternoon, I'd take the girls back to their home to be reunited with their parents, hopefully giving their mother enough time to do her own thing, either around the house or shopping or whatever she might like to do. It was free time for Terry!

We followed this family routine for eight to ten years, until the girls became involved with athletics and clubs at school, ending our exclusive Saturday adventures. While it was a bit sad for me, it marked a new phase of going to see the girls play sports and excel and grow with their various teams. I came to enjoy watching their soccer matches and track meets, becoming an avid supporter and cheerleader from the sidelines.

Morgan emerged as a track star, becoming a big time competitor at the University of North Carolina when she reached college age, earning trophies and honors with some of the nation's best athletes. She was only repeating the honors she had garnered at Harpeth Hall.

Mary pursued art and became honored for her skills and creativity. She did beautiful paintings, drawings and sculptures, as well as other art projects both at Harpeth Hall and at college at the University of Texas at Austin, as well as on her own.

Sara is, as this memoir is being written, a student at the University of Alabama in Tuscaloosa, taking pre-nursing courses. I hope to see more of her should she be enrolled at a nursing school next year. Time will tell.

What can I say, I am truly blessed!

In the meantime, my middle son Christian moved to Africa, after spending time in Tasmania. He joined the Peace Corps, after perfecting French at the University of Lausanne in Switzerland. He had to be fluent in two languages to serve in the Corps. His first assignment was in the west African nation of Togo. He chose the uppermost post available in Togo. The other Peace Corps workers wanted to be near the Togo coastline, which is the most populous area of the country. Chris' mind didn't work that way. He is very serious and deeply committed to the work he does, so he went where the aid was most needed. The good people of Togo didn't want to see Christian leave after the usual 24 months to which a Peace Corps volunteer commits. After serving his two years in Togo, the villagers signed a petition which they sent to the Peace Corps organization requesting that Christian Stengel be allowed to extend his stay in Togo for another 12 months. Permission was granted. Under Christian's stay in Togo, he was able to get financing for much needed roads and other infrastructures in their village. Oxen were purchased to help plow the fields instead of plowing by hand As part of his training, Christian spent time on a farm as arranged with Lafond cousins in Quebec.

Later he went to work for various NGOs (Non-Governmental Organizations) moving around Africa and living in many African countries.

He married Charlotte Mutarigirwa from Rwanda, where he now lives. He met her right after the genocide in April 1994 in Rwanda. She lived through it and experienced first-hand, the horrors of that conflict. Christian was not in Rwanda at the time of the genocide. My daughter-in-law Charlotte is a brave heart, a brave soul, and a wonderful woman. We've become very good friends and I truly love her, as I love Terry, Marc's wife. I share the same middle name as Christian's wife, Charlotte.

My youngest son, Eric was married to Claudia Knauer, and they are now divorced. They have two darling daughters, August (A.K.) who is now 15, and Marie who will be 11 on New Year's Eve, this year, 2012. They are both wonderful girls who are doing extremely well at Currey-Ingram Academy. August is on the Deans list and has a 4.0 average in all academics. She is also taking some college courses. I just wish I could see them more often. They see their dad every other weekend, and I don't want to infringe on their times with him. When they are a bit older, perhaps that will be possible.

I know that August does horseback riding after school and on weekends and is very involved with the sport. Marie is active in gymnastics. She loves it and is very good at it, from what her Dad tells me.

I had a special treat last summer of 2012 when Christian, Charlotte and their two daughters, Zoe, age 14, and Kaia, age 11, came from Rwanda, Africa for a 2 month visit. They arrived on June 4th and left on August 5th. It was wonderful having them in Nashville. I found a furnished apartment for them in Green Hills within walking distance of Kroger, Whole Foods and Trader Joe's. They were also close to the Mall at Green Hills, which was very convenient for them, and everybody concerned. It was great fun having the African contingent of the Lafond/Stengel family gathered together for two entire months.

Marc, Suzanne, Claudia, Eric, Kermit and Christian Stengel, on Eric's wedding day. Photo taken at Scarrit Chapel, Nashville.

The Stengel Brothers on Eric and Claudia's wedding day

Marc and Suzanne at Eric's wedding day festivities

Marc and his dad at the wedding reception for Eric and Claudia in the clubhouse at Arden Place

Pierre Lafond in Nashville for Eric and Claudia Stengel's wedding. Seen here with his much younger sister, Suzanne!

Terry Stengel admiring her first born, Mary

*Contented Granddaddy, Kermit Stengel with
Marc and Terry's first daughter, Mary*

Marc Stengel and his girls, all wearing tiaras. From left: Baby Sara on Marc's lap, Suzanne, Mary behind Marc, and Morgan, all in Mamie's house

Mary, Morgan and Sara recreating the popular toboggan seating arrangement used in the past by their dad and uncles.

The cover girls of the day! Helen's Children Shop used Morgan, Sara and Mary Stengel as their models for an ad in the newspaper at Christmas time. The photo was taken by Bet Scott, a fellow Canadian, by the way.

Sara Sudekum Stengel and her Teddy Bear

Peach Cobbler Stories

*Mary, Sara and Morgan Stengel framed
in the hollow of a very large tree!*

Washington State Apple Commission Promo Photo taken by Marc Stengel for the Search for Granny Smith competition. From left: Mary, Morgan and Sara Stengel pictured with their grandmother, Suzanne Lafond, a candidate, and the eventual winner of the contest.

From left: Morgan, Mary and Sara Stengel

Terry and Marc Stengel and their daughters: First row left: Terry, Morgan and her protector, Wiley. Back row left: Marc, Sara and Mary

Marc and Terry Stengel family photos
First photo upper left: Terry, Mary and Marc Stengel,
Top upper right photo: Mary, Middle photo: Sara Stengel,
Bottom left photo:Morgan in a track meet at the University of
North Carolina, Bottom right photo: three sisters: Sara, Mary and
Morgan Stengel

August Knauer Stengel and Marie Woolwine Stengel

Peach Cobbler Stories

August K. Stengel and Marie W. Stengel, daughters of Claudia and Eric Stengel

Marie at the window of their dollhouse and August in the doorway, daughters of Claudia and Eric Stengel

Middle School Graduation Day at Currey Ingram Academy in June 2012. Eric and Claudia's daughters: August and Marie on a warm and sunny day with their Mamie. Suzanne notes: "I must mention that AK wore the most beautiful, soft pink dress for her graduation, the prettiest dress I had ever seen on a young girl. I wish I could show it to you. AK felt more comfortable in the relaxed clothes in which she is pictured above. Both AK and Marie are the smartest and prettiest girls on the Currey Ingram Academy campus" says their Mamie!

Eric Lafond Stengel in a triathlete competition

Eric and his glider, waiting to be towed aloft at John Tune Airport, Nashville

Suzanne piloting Eric's glider

Christian Stengel and his family: Zoelie, Christian, Kaia and Charlotte

Zoelie's first trip to the USA at 9 months of age, with her mother Charlotte Stengel

Zoelie Stengel, oldest daughter of Christian and Charlotte Stengel

Granddaughter Kaia Stengel, daughter of Charlotte Mutarigirwa and Christian Stengel

Peach Cobbler Stories

A spontaneous use of water colors by mother and son. Suzanne's art on top and Eric's birthday card below.

A Sudden Summer Rain

Ashley Benton sat on the back steps of her parents' country house lacing up her hiking boots. She thought of the woods she wanted to explore, perhaps have lunch by the lake and climb the hills surrounding it. It was a glorious day! The kind of day which forces you out of the house and hands you a gift at every turn. Everywhere she looked the sun splashed the landscape brilliantly. How she loved being out of doors!

Ashley was fourteen, strong and athletic. She liked sports more than almost anything she could think of. She had been born with keen coordination and a fine set of muscles. In the words of her school coaches, she was "talented." As she sat there, she pondered for a moment whether she should ask her little sister to go with her.

Mimi was almost twelve and small for her age. She was frail looking, but she was very bright, quick and full of energy. What she lacked in athletic ability she more than made up in scholastic achievements.

"Hey squirt, how would you like to go hiking with me today?" Ashley called out to her sister who was dashing through the kitchen.

"You mean it, Ashley?" she questioned, then added "Sure I'd like to go, are you leaving now?...Wait a minute while I ask Mom" she hurried so Ashley wouldn't have time to change her mind. She was thrilled to have been asked to go with her big sister.

While Mimi went looking for their mother, Ashley began preparing lunch for their hike. A picnic in a field or by a lake or in the mountains made everything taste ten times better. Mrs. Benton cautioned Ashley to keep an eye out for Mimi.

"Don't worry about a thing, Mom, we'll be fine. We are IN CONTROL aren't we Mimi?" she teased.

"That's right Mom, we are IN CONTROL," she echoed.

The girls ran out leaping and skipping their way along the road. Soon they entered a beautifully wooded area where the tree branches formed a canopy over their heads. Just as Ashley was wondering about the many different kinds of trees, Mimi volunteered that the clump of trees just ahead were silver maples.

"How can you tell?" asked Ashley.

"The easiest way is by looking at the leaves. Silver maples have a whitened look, their leaves have five points, like this one, you see, it is a bit hairy underneath." Mimi handed Ashley the leaf. "Also" she said, "The bark of a young silver maple is smooth and gray, while an older tree, like that one over there, has flaking bark which leaves brown spots as it falls off."

"That's really amazing," Ashley said.

"There are other kinds of maples too, I'll show them to you as we meet up with them," Mimi added.

"Tell me about those on the other side of the path, Mimi," asked Ashley.

"They are white oaks. You can tell because their leaves are long and narrow with lots of fingers on both sides of the spine" and turning the leaf, Mimi added "Very often, the underside of the leaf is whitened". Mimi showed Ashley that the bark was ashy-gray and scaly.

"I wish I knew more about growing things, like you do Mimi," Ashley said pensively.

"Well, if you like, I'll teach you what I know and you can coach me in sports and games," Mimi suggested.

"That's a deal, squirt?" Ashley answered with laughter in her voice. Along the path, Mimi pointed out teaberry leaves and their reddish, spicy berries. "Teaberry leaves are sometimes used to make tea, I've tried some and it has a clean fresh taste - like they say in some commercials," Mimi joked.

There were some wild mushrooms along the way also, but Mimi didn't know which were safe to eat and which were poisonous, so she didn't pick any. They saw many beautiful ferns and velvety moss which Mimi said grew on the north side of trees.

When they reached Frenchman's Lake, Ashley decided it would be a fine place to have lunch. Off came the hiking boots and they plunged their hot tired feet into the lake. The lake was cold as most lake waters are, but it felt good to wiggle their toes in the water. After lunch, Mimi pulled something from her pocket, which had been wrapped in a big heart shaped linden leaf. She unfolded her treasure carefully and there were small, baby sized strawberries glistening in the sunlight.

"How pretty those things are, but what are they?" Ashley asked.

"These are wild strawberries, found in the woods" Mimi said. In French they are called "Fraises des bois." "Try one and see how sweet they are," Mimi offered.

"They're safe to eat too," Mimi added.

"They are WONDERFUL, the sweetest I've ever tasted," declared Ashley.

They sat on a warm rock sunning themselves like chameleons and talked. It was a good time for sisters to get to know each other a little better. The differences between them seemed to matter not one whit. In fact, they began to think that they could learn so much from one another."

"All right, let's get going," Ashley announced.

"Last one to the big rock over there is a toad," said Ashley laughing.

Mimi could never beat Ashley in a race of any kind. Somehow it didn't seem to matter so much anymore.

Suddenly, storm clouds were gathering above their heads. Before they realized it, there was a bolt of lightning followed closely by a thunder clap. Ashley and her sister went scurrying for cover. Ashley knew it was unsafe to stand beneath a tree during a storm, so they looked for better shelter. Nearby, they saw what appeared to be an old abandoned house.

"Come on, let's make a run for it," Ashley said.

In a dash they ran across a clearing and jumped up on the porch of the old house.

"Boy, that was close, we're just in time. Will you look at that sky?" Ashley pointed to the clouds.

"It looks like the lightning splits the sky in two," Ashley said excitedly.

Then Ashley began counting: "One thousand and one, one thousand and two, one thousand and three, one thousand and four..."

"What are you doing, Ashley?" Mimi was wondering.

"Well, if you count slowly just that way, from the time you see the flash of lightning in the sky until you hear the rumble of thunder, it will tell you how far the storm is," explained Ashley.

"How's that?" asked Mimi.

"Each count is supposed to represent one mile, so right now the storm is about 18 miles away," Ashley answered.

"Who told you that?" Mimi looked doubtful.

"Mr. Cooper, you know, the man who owns the farm next to the village, he told me that," said Ashley. "Do you believe that Ashley?"

"Well, I don't know how scientific it is, but it helps me to not be afraid of thunder and lightning when I count. It's kind of a trick, I guess. It takes your mind off the scary parts when there is a storm."

"Well, we beat the rain, alright, look at it now, it is coming down in sheets," said Ashley.

In a way, it was a wonderful summer storm. There is a special light in the sky during summer rains. Even the lightning and thunder were kind of exciting to Ashley. Maybe it had to do with all that electricity bumping about in the clouds which was energizing everyone around.

Ashley put down her back pack and with both hands, she pushed open the heavy wooden door. It squeaked as she did so, probably because no one had been around for a while. It had big rusty lead hinges which seemed to be crying for oil. Once inside, Ashley's eyes adjusted to the darkness and she saw a couple of lopsided chairs, a rickety table and a small well-worn bench. She heard Mimi mutter something about the funny smell in here, to which Ashley replied: "That's just a musty smell, abandoned houses get funny smelling that way. Houses aren't meant to be empty. Even small ones in the woods."

"Let's find scraps of wood and some paper to build a fire in the fireplace," suggested Ashley. "I brought matches in my little metal matchbox, and plenty of them," she said.

Even though she was busying about, gathering wood, building the fire, arranging the chairs near the fire, Ashley wasn't completely at ease in this old house. It was a little like whistling in the dark when you're afraid of the darkness.

As they watched the fire, enjoying it's warmth and the smell of burning logs, they were startled by a man's deep and booming voice coming through the open door.

The voice said: "Who's in there?"

Ashley, frozen in fear, said nothing.

The male voice continued: "Whoever you are, you had better come out before I come in and get you out."

"Oh m'gosh, Mimi, we had better show our faces," Ashley said.

As the two sisters peered from behind the door, the man who belonged to the voice gave a long hearty laugh. "Don't look so scared" he said, "I own this land and this old house, so when I saw smoke coming out the chimney, I had to investigate," he tried to reassure them.

Fritz Steiner was the man's name and he lived on this huge farm. He had come on horseback because it was too muddy for a car and too wet to come on foot. He told the girls that the creek they'd have to cross to get back to the village was overflowing and you couldn't get across on foot.

"What should we do?" asked Ashley. "By the way, Mr. Steiner, my name is Ashley Benton and this is my sister Mimi," she added.

"The first thing to do is put out the fire in the fireplace, then you can ride back with me on my horse Patrick," said Mr. Steiner.

The three of them had a safe ride back to the village. Mr. Steiner had been right about the creek, Ashley thought. It was very deep now and the current quite swift. They would not have been able to cross it on foot, that's for sure.

Fritz Steiner, who had so frightened Ashley back at the old house, turned out to be a very nice man. He knew the Bentons, although had not met the daughters until now. He had, in fact, heard that the two girls had gone hiking in the direction of his property and thought he would have a look about his property when he saw the storm coming up so suddenly.

"It was kind of you to come looking for us in the rain, Mr. Steiner" Ashley said as she shook his hand. "Goodbye and thanks a million."

"You'll not soon forget the sudden summer rains we have out here," Mr. Steiner said smiling.

The day wasn't ruined by the rain. It had given them a bit of an adventure they would not otherwise have experienced. It was the kind of stuff around which tall tales could be told, thought Ashley.

*A street scene in art class painted
by Suzanne Lafond in Nashville, TN*

*A landscape scene in art class painted by Suzanne Lafond at
l' Ecole des Beaux Arts de Montréal*

Le Week-End

Jacqueline Benoit was born in Paris and in all her twelve years she has never left France. She has travelled outside of Paris to two or three other cities and has even spent several weeks in the south of France during summer holidays, but that was as far as she has ever been.

Jacqueline's father made arrangements for her to spend a year with relatives in America because Jacqueline's mother was recovering from a serious illness. Jacqueline did not know her American relatives very well. She had met them six years ago when she was only six. She knew that her cousin Stephen was fourteen years old and that he had a sister, Louise, who was almost eight.

So it was really like meeting them all again for the first time. Jacqueline wondered what Stephen would be like. Did he speak French at all? Would he be impatient with her school-girl English. She didn't feel comfortable speaking English outside the classroom. She had never spoken English to real English speaking people like Americans. Perhaps Stephen was asking himself some of the same questions about her. He probably wondered how well she would fit in with his American friends - would they understand her? Would her ways be different from what he was used to with his friends?

Well, Jacqueline was about to find the answers to those questions. After months and weeks of anticipation, she was flying to Summerville this Friday. Her plane was arriving at seven o'clock in the evening. Stephen Landon and his family were going to be there to meet her plane. As the passengers ahead of her reached the gate Jacqueline peered around them trying to locate her American relatives. She spotted a very handsome young boy who looked to be about the same age as her cousin and she decided that it was

Stephen. He was tall, dark hair and eyes and his face broke into a big smile when he spotted her. She had been right. This was her cousin Stephen Landon.

He approached her tentatively.

"Jacqueline? Is your name Jacqueline?"

A warm smile spread across Jacqueline's face.

"Yes, are you Stephen?"

They shook hands, pleased to have found one another so easily. Laughingly, Jacqueline said "Bonsoir, Stephane."

Stephen asked: "Does that mean good evening?" With a twinkle in her eye she answered "Oui."

"What fun this will be," said Stephen. "You can teach me to speak French and I will help you with English."

She beamed and replied "d'accord."

Jacqueline spoke better English than she realized. All those classroom conversations were paying off in real life. Stephen laughed at the way she rearranged the emphasis on certain syllables in a lot of words. He said he thought it was 'verrrree sharming' assuming something of a French accent himself. He added: "If I have to answer to Stephane, then you will have to get used to being called Jackie."

"I like that" she said. Suddenly, Jackie's new surroundings, the new town, the newly met cousin seemed reassuringly exciting. This was the beginning of a great adventure. She made up her mind then and there, that this would not be an ordeal, a dreaded time away from her sick mother and her father. This really was a privilege, if she thought about it, and a great learning experience. Her mother would get well, she was sure of that, and after spending a school year with her American relatives, she would take back to France so many unique and exciting stories. She would surely be the envy of her French classmates.

One thing she learned right away, was that it would be quite different not having to go to school on Saturdays. "Le weekend" was a wonderful American invention. In France, Thursdays were a day off and Saturdays were school days.

As it turned out, this first weekend in Summerville was filled with exciting plans. Jackie and Stephen would be dropped off at Moon Drugstore where Stephen was to meet his school chums and, as a group, they would walk a short distance to their school. Stephen's high school football team was playing an important game that day. He was very helpful in explaining the difference between American football and French football, which is known as soccer to Americans.

Saturday, Jackie and Stephen made plans to ride bicycles to a nearby lake to meet friends and have a picnic lunch in one of the state parks along the way. The weather was still warm, the air was clear and the leaves were ever so slowly changing colors. Autumn was beautiful in America, Jackie thought.

At a fork in the road, Jackie, Stephen and two friends from the group, decided to go left. The others followed the right fork and were a few minutes ahead of Stephen. Stephen knew the left trail led to a stream. The stream, in fact, separated the trail. Stephen and his friends had often crossed it on their bikes. Usually, the current was gentle, if there was any at all, and the water quite shallow.

Today however, because there had been some hard rains and stormy days recently, the stream seemed fuller than Stephen remembered it. They all agreed that it couldn't be that deep or the current that strong, just because of a few rainy days and so they began their descent into the water while riding their bikes.

Jackie and the two friends, Bill and Mike, crossed the stream with great difficulty because the current proved to be quite strong and the water was halfway up their bicycle wheels. They were drenched up to their knees. Stephen, surveying the situation, decided to make a run for it by pedaling very hard from the top of the hill to the water, sailing through the water at great speed. What he didn't count on was the slipperiness of the flat rock he had to cross on the way to the other side. And so, at a very fast clip, and with no traction, Stephen went flying off his bike and was thrown a few feet downstream. Before anyone could react, Stephen was being carried away by the swift current.

Mike, Bill and Jackie were in a panic. They all yelled at once. Help! help! and au secours! au secours! They ran on the bank alongside the stream, trying to catch up with Stephen who was being swept away. They had a terrible time going around, under and over all the brush on the bank of the stream. They worried that Stephen might have hit his head on a rock or a boulder along the way and might be unconscious. In a matter of seconds, Mike and Bill knew it could be all over because there were falls where the stream plunged nearly fifty feet, just a sort distance from where they stood now.

Jackie kept calling "Stephane, Stephane, répond-moi." All knowledge of English seemed to have gone out of her head at the moment. She could only call out in French her anguish for Stephane's welfare.

Suddenly, as if an answer to a prayer, they spotted a huge boulder knocked down by the recent storms which had fallen across the stream right in front of the falls. It blocked the path of the swift current and kept Stephen from falling to the rocks below. They could now see that he was not unconscious and he held on for dear life to the boulder which had saved him from the falls.

Soon, his friends and Jackie, caught up with him. Carefully inching toward the water, they handed him a freshly fallen tree limb, with the leaves still on the branches. Stephen, exhausted by his struggle, managed to grab first the leaves, then inching up, he grabbed the branches. He held onto that limb until he was within easy reach of Jackie's extended arm, while Bill and Mike were stabilizing the tree limb as best they could.

Jackie, with tears in her eyes kept repeating Stephen's name "Stephane, Stephane comment es-tu? Es-tu blessé? Que tu es courageux! Quel miracle!" She thought that it was indeed a miracle that he wasn't carried over the falls. What had begun as a beautiful bicycle ride on a weekend afternoon turned out to be a near tragedy. She would never forget how frightened she had been for Stephane.

The rest of the bicycle party appeared on the scene. They had turned back a short distance after the fork in the road because they didn't see their friends behind them and thought they heard Bill, Mike and Jackie calling for help.

Other than a few bruises, cuts and scrapes, Stephen was badly shaken, but quite able to get around on his own if wobbly legs.

Stephen, Jackie, Bill and Mike retrieved their bicycles from where the mishap occurred and picked up the trail from the other side of the river. Not wanting to take a chance crossing the stream, the rest of the friends agreed to meet the four at the start of the trail.

On the way home, they discussed whether they should tell the Landons of their adventure and they thought it best that they should. On the other hand, because Jacqueline's family was an ocean away and her mother still recovering from her illness, it was decided that recounting this adventure could wait until she got home after the school year.

There were more week-ends to plan for, more experiences to be shared with her cousin, but Jacqueline hoped that no other should be quite as frightening as this one. Jacqueline thought this introduction to American life would be indelibly linked in her mind to her first "WeekEnd" in Somerville.

Painting by Léa Lafond

Renée Castagnola, from Santa Barbara, called Suzanne in January, 1990, to propose a five week trip to Central and Eastern Europe. She wanted to know if Suzanne could be ready by the fifth of February. How they achieved this with visas and the rest of the details the trip entailed is a miracle, but they did it! They picked up a Volkswagen Passat in Frankfurt, then traveled to Spain, Yugoslavia, Bulgaria, Hungary and Czechoslovakia, before returning to Germany for the flight back to the USA. Suzanne wrote an article about the trip for a small Catholic newspaper.

Scenic trip photo in Yugoslavia

The Secret

It is so nice to know that Mary Elizabeth and Morgan like to have lunch at my house after our Saturday morning outing. More often than not, we attend Davis-Kidd Booksellers' story hour (which is really on the shy side of 30 minutes), then I give them a choice of places to go for lunch. Almost always it's "Your house, Mamie." I am usually prepared for that, but I like the idea of giving them choices.

One Saturday, after Mary Elizabeth's soccer practice, I invited her to stop by my house for lunch. Morgan had a little cold so she didn't go to the practice field with Mary Elizabeth and her Daddy. And so, back we came to A-R-D-E-N P-L-A-C-E (that's the way we pronounce it as we drive in, to make the name clear to them), and we sat down to a small lunch. At one point Mary Elizabeth said something about "The Baby." At first, it didn't register with me, but immediately, Mary Elizabeth flushed and looked genuinely distressed that she had let this slip so quickly and unintentionally. She covered her mouth and began to whisper even though we were alone in the house. She allowed that her mommy was going to have a baby, but it was a secret and she wasn't supposed to tell. I assured her that it would be our secret... to which she added that it was her mommy's and her daddy's secret too!

And so that is how I came to find out that the little Stengel family of four would have five come May of 1991. I am thrilled for all of us. Marc and Terry, who have wanted to add to their family, are very excited too. All these important events in my own son's life reaffirm so positively my decision to return to live in Nashville in the Fall of 1988. I came to be near grand children and as far as I am concerned, the more the better!

Haute Comme Trois Pommes

She was only as tall as three apples! That's how we measure small children in French. Meaning she was a wee little thing!

It was a crisp October morning ... the kind of day you know that by noon you will shed your warm sweater.

Small family clumps dotted the sideline, ready to applaud their David or Adam or Peter, or as in our case, Mary Elizabeth playing in her very first soccer match. The frightened, seemingly timid little blond girl stood by herself, awed by the energy and zip of all those boys darting about the field. At times she took small skipping steps to join them, other times she watched while chewing on one of her fingers. Not too excited by this first contest. The very first such in all of her five years. Mary Elizabeth, by the way, probably measured five or six apples high by then.

The one who was only three apples tall is named Morgan. She is the little sister of the soccer player. When I first spotted her on the edge of the field that day, the sun danced on her light auburn hair and her cheeks were of a pink seen only on little girls' faces... especially if they are only three apples high!

I joined my family clump, and Morgan looked around, with the broadest smile I have ever seen. She squealed with joy and let out a "Mamie!" that made my heart leap.

A "Mamie!" you know has an exclamation point all built in and with that she flew into my outstretched arms. At the risk of sounding corny, I want to say that I cannot describe the joy I felt at the reception I received. We cradled one another in the biggest hug this little girl could possibly give. She then looked into my eyes and began taking an inventory of my face: "Mamie's" eyes, my cheeks, my mouth, my spectacles, all the while giggling and chatting inconsequentially, as two year olds are want to do. I looked at her with my heart on my sleeve and was struck at how pure and innocent she was. Truly one of God's littlest angels.

Mary Elizabeth did not see much action on the playing field that day. You see, she feigned a stomach ache so she could get out of the game. I think the other team won, but the little boys certainly looked like they were having great fun, no matter which side scored.

Mary Elizabeth and her Dad walked home hand in hand from Julia Green school. It would give him a chance to talk about the game with Mary Elizabeth, Marc said.

Morgan cried when she was told she could not come to my house because of other plans her mommy and daddy had made for them that afternoon. As a small compromise, we all decided I could take Morgan with me for some juice and a bite of lunch and bring her back in time for them to go ahead with their plans.

What a soft little girl she is; it is fun to talk to her now because there is so much she can talk about. What a dear and tender age. So easily scooped up and hugged. I love to watch her as she runs or walks or plays, she is after all only as high as three apples. "Haute comme trois pommes!"

You Don't Have To Wear Your Wedding Dress

We were rounding the corner, Mary Elizabeth seated next to me in the front seat and Morgan in the back, when Kermit's house came into view on Gerald Place.

Mary Elizabeth pointed to the house and said: "That's grandfather's and Pat's house." I hit on the opportunity to mention that I, too, had lived in that house. " In fact, Mary Elizabeth," I said, "Your grandfather and I built that house." She seemed astonished to hear that and said "You did, Mamie?" all the while placing her hands on her hips and looking incredulous. "I didn't know that," she added.

And now, as if a light bulb had turned on in her head, she proposed enthusiastically: "Mamie, the next time we go for a visit, you should come with us." "Oh, I don't think that would be a very good idea, sweetheart" I said. "Why, Mamie?" she asked. "Well, your grandfather is married to Pat now and I can't drop by for a visit," I explained lamely. Impatient with my reasoning, Mary Elizabeth looked at me intensely and said with her hands on her hips: "Mamie, you don't have to wear your wedding dress!" Problem solved!

Mary Elizabeth Stengel had just turned 5 on April 15, 1990.

A Victory

Today, Saturday, July 21, 1990, Mary Elizabeth Stengel tasted a victory. One of many, I predict.

It happened at the Arden Place swimming pool. Mary Elizabeth learned to swim. Oh, she had been pretending for some time now, but I mean true, honest to goodness swimming from the shallow end to the deep end of the swimming pool. Her daddy swam alongside of her, encouraging her stroke by stroke, until she reached the deep end.

It was positively thrilling.

This was the same little girl who six weeks earlier balked at putting her head in the water. I was so proud and excited for her.

Whatever connection needed to be made was made today and she turned the corner, so to speak.

That she learned to swim at age five is not in itself the most spectacular aspect of the day. Many children swim at a much earlier age. The real feat is that she conquered her fear of the water, or at least tamed it. That was the true victory.

A Poet You Are Not!

That is correct, I do not deserve the title of poet. I never studied the art of Poetry, never published poems…maybe one…long ago.

Please don't tell my heart, because I believe in the most fundamental core of any one of us, poetry exists. For me it is the soul that spills its contents onto the page. Maybe it is a way to relieve a build-up of thoughts, or soothe an ache, then again words find their way on the page due to unshed tears of sadness, of love, of what has been and will never be again…or simply of things that move me.

Papa reminded me that the future was full of promise…Is it? There is so little future left…but when Papa said it, it was full of promise. He didn't say only if one is thirty years old!

Papa's daughter,
Suzanne Charlotte Lafond
April 2013

I Think I Am A Poet

February 2, 1986

I am a poet!
My poems have never been published
Some have never been written
Or spoken
How then can I call myself a poet, you ask? Because so many of my thoughts are born
In that part of one's soul reserved for poems
It is a deep well content to be still, mostly dark with patches of sunlight
But which, on occasion, bubbles up to the surface and lands squarely on a page
A crystallized thought embodied in words, a message of the spirit to be held onto
To be thought again
Yes, I am a poet!

Suzanne

Chez André – The Shrine – Montréal

I wandered, exhausted, into a small café
On an afternoon of museum visits.
The prospect of espresso and a chair
Were uppermost in my mind.
How familiar the place seemed to be
I looked up at the sound of a deep hello!
The basso profundo voice called my name "Is that you Suzy?"
Yes, it is I
Is it really you Norman?
How can this be when we've not seen one another in over forty years?
I came for a visit…and there you are!
Of course I remember Chez André,
We called it The Shrine because of the "Oratoire Saint Joseph" where
Brother André performed so many miracles
We spent many hours in this place
It has changed, we've changed too
Not so much that we wouldn't recognize one another.
Has life been good to you, Norman?
Have you been happy?
As happy as we were in those carefree days?
I've thought of you so many times
Do you remember Sadie Hawkins Day?
Are you aware of the courage it took to ask you to the dance?
You were bashful, shy even.
Would we be together now, had we not been seventeen?
We were on the threshold of life, before it unfurled.
It is said that every relationship has to grow or die.
I don't know that ours would have grown
But the fickle temperament of youth
Let it die.

Suzanne Lafond   June 14, 1995

The Night Visitor

He came at night, mostly, to look through my window
He stretched out in the most disjointed way
On the wall separating my house from the neighbor's
We became nodding acquaintances
Often, he was still there in the morning, when I opened the shutters
Gradually, we became friends, distant ones, to be sure, but we were friends
He even dared to sleep on the outdoor chairs
Or on my doorstep
He chanced to speak when he eyed me through the window
Or when I fetched the mail
I knew not his name, nor where he lived, nor how he felt,
He stopped coming quite suddenly
I missed him, but was not alarmed
Until late one evening when returning home, the headlights of my car
Shone on a small, broken, furry animal.
The victim of a machine he could not know was an enemy
In death as in life, my nightly visitor, a black and white cat,
Was stretched out in the most disjointed way.

Suzanne Lafond

Letting Go

Letting go of mother's breast, father's hand,
And Teddy Bear.
Of a teacher's guidance, family ties
And the nest.
Of your children's lives of a relationship
Of all past dreams
Of one's youth
Of false pride
Of deep sighs
Of gossip about self
Of wanting the last word of insisting you are right
When you know you are!
Of all that is unimportant
Of lost wealth
Of protestations
Petty jealousies
Small thoughts and your turn
Just let it go, let it go.
Only then can you grow
When you learn to let go

Suzanne, November 1997

Letting Go

Version Two

I have been thinking of all the times we let go of so many things, people and places
Letting go, I've decided, is a huge part of life, but that doesn't make it easy. Letting go of mother's breast, father's hand and Teddy Bear
Of a teacher's guidance.
Of family ties and the family nest,
Of your children's love.
Letting go of a close relationship
Which is full of promise and scarcely begun
Because you know in your wisdom that it would never be right.
Letting go of romantic dreams,
Of walks and talks and sharing life. Letting go of present and future joys
Of promises hoped for and hopes never promised.
Letting go can seem so tragic, so irreversibly final.
Are we allowed one or two beautiful dreams?
Sure we are, lest all dreams cease!

My Sixty Years

October 9, 1989

Looking back on my life, I began to play with the numbers that make up my sixty years on earth.

I have seen the light of day 21,900 times. It seems like a lot. Pretty remarkable, actually.

Even more remarkable, though is that my heart has beaten 1,892,160,000 steady, mostly reassuring heartbeats. Along with everything else that has gone on in my efficient machine, that in itself is a cause for celebration.

No parts have had to be replaced. Certainly our man-made machinery is not nearly so dependable.

Sixty years isn't so very long when I count the things I have yet to do and see and hear.

I want the time to be able to see Marc, Terry, Mary Elizabeth, Morgan and Sara financially more comfortable. I hope to see my granddaughters grown and settled in the pursuit of their lives.

I would like to know that Christian is safe, happy and fulfilled in the life he has chosen in the developing world. I wish for him the right person to complement his chosen path. It will take an extraordinary woman, but I am confident that someone exists, just for him. And of course, I hope he too will have children for me to love and hold and eventually see them grow up to be successful human beings, like their mom and dad.   .

I wish for Eric and Claudia great success in their chosen careers. Between the two and separately, there is so much creative talent waiting to be let out. I want that talent recognized and respected. I hope that their many dreams and ideas see fruition. I would like to see their financial burdens become a thing of the past, so that they might concentrate on creating. And eventually, like Marc and Christian, I hope they too will know the joys of parenthood. They must know it.

Perhaps I will see the day when Marc's many talents will also be recognized. Life need not be so difficult for him and his little family. A successful book or play or short story could buy him the time he needs to devote to writing full time.

In a word, I want for each of my sons what they want. My wish is to be around when they either reach their goals or are on the road that leads them there.

I pray that Terry stays happy with Marc and with their life together. Terry and Claudia are wonderful daughters. I could not have picked better wives for either of them if I had been asked to.

The Whale Rider

Well, here it is July 24, 2005.

I have just finished watching *The Whale Rider* on PBS. A profound sadness engulfed me as I became more and more drawn into the story. It is beautiful story. The courage and determination of a young girl to gain the acceptance of her gruff grandfather and to prove herself to her ancestors and her community was inspiring. For some reason, it took me back to my days with my father; strong and at times intimidating, but loving and gentle at his best. How powerful he seemed to me in all the summers I spent at Camp le Capitaine. He was after all, Le Grand Manitou, the Big Chief of this camping community. I miss Rodolphe and Lea immensely; every day of my life. What we had, what we could have had. It leaves a gaping hole in my heart to think that I lost them both so young — papa was 58, maman was 69 and I was 28 and 38 at their deaths. I am very sad as I write this. I have outlived them both at age 74.

The Whale Rider not only made me sad and tearful, but my heart hurts atrociously tonight. I must remember the young girl's courage and that inspires me to sit up straight and remember how strong I am. I do have backbone, I have a strength and a determination that surprises even me. What I must do with my pulpy heart is to determine not to be broken by life and its challenges. I thrust my shoulders back, dry my tears and face tomorrow with energy and vigor.

Physical activity has always been a big coping mechanism for me. I maintain that we can control the thoughts that come into our brain. It is an exercise I practice often. Obviously, I have always liked being in charge of my life. I was a victim for a time in the latter years of my marriage to Kermit, but leaving him restored my self-confidence. Living with Kermit can be described simply as "his way or the highway." At times I felt like his employee, not his partner. I am forced to remember that he who has the money has the power. Kermit exercised power seamlessly. Mostly, I think of Kermit, not as a bad guy, but as an emotional cripple who had no role model in either parent, but perhaps more to the point, deep in his inherited genes. The Teutonic traits made up who he is. I was happy in my marriage for 12 to 15 years, perhaps more. However, in the last ten years I felt more and more miserable. I thought if I didn't do something about it, I would die young. My own spirit was dying. Kermit never talked to me, he had his own pursuits. He once told me that his favorite things were 1. Playing tennis 2. Cutting the grass 3. Work at Kermit C. Stengel, Jr. Co. Nothing more, no mention of his wife and children. I wanted to scream, but I simply turned and walked away; my heart was bleeding inside my chest. In short, Kermit seemed to shut down completely where his domestic life was concerned. What empty and desperately lonely feelings I had.

I am at the threshold of a partnership with Dress for Success and Goodwill and I must be wise, sharp, careful and be the strong negotiator I know myself to be. So much is at stake. If there is a succession plan for DFS, this has to be it. Otherwise, when I step away, as I know I must, without a solid arrangement with Goodwill, it would spell the end of my seven year venture. I have worked hard and have energy and the will to go on, but now I am working toward this partnership so as to ensure a succession for DFS Nashville, whenever I step down or continue.

Pierre once asked me, as we rode together to San Ynez to visit his vineyards, what I thought made me so strong. I reflected for a while and said that my ancestors make me strong. The courage they, and many like them, displayed in leaving France for the new world - not knowing where, what, how, they would live - is one of the highest examples of courage I can think of where family matters are concerned. The women were strong. They were survivors, capable, intelligent women who must have been extremely resourceful. How often I wish I could have met all of them and talked about all this. How wonderful it would be to share a meal with all those who came before us. Would I like them, would I be proud of them, would they like me, would they be proud of me?

Another deep sadness that I rarely voice, is the fact that Marc and Eric, who live no further than 2-4 miles from me, seem to forget that I exist. I know (and well remember) how little time I had for my own mother when she lived in Nashville, a period I shall always remember with regret. But a telephone call once a week doesn't seem such a difficult or demanding request. I don't make that request, for it would be followed by an avalanche of excuses, impatience and even anger by either Marc or Eric.

Life is far too busy for family connections to exist as one anticipates they will. After all, if anyone understands, I do. They have their work, their families, their friends, their concerns, their occupations, their lives.

I regroup my thoughts all the time and lower my expectations in the hope that I will not be so sad. It is very difficult. Everyone tells me that is the way of sons. Girls are more attentive to their own mothers and sometimes daughters-in-law take up the slack. I attempted that with Kermit's mother.

I accept what I cannot change and thank God that he has given me good health and the ability to take two steps forward when I take one step back. I am always hoping for pathetic little crumbs and I am so happy when they fall in my lap! Perhaps it is all a testament to my not being the good mother I thought I was. I really thought I was. Dear God! Wasn't I? Have I failed?

My Place

It is a wee place I now call home
It is filled with street noises, flowers, music
sunshine and light
A glimpse of the ocean through the trees
But mostly it is filled with peace
It is just big enough to enclose me
My world is much smaller now
My world is in my soul
My first residence in Santa Barbara after leaving Nashville
where I lived for 25 years, was on Middle Rd. in Montecito.
I was there for only one year.

Suzanne Lafond
May 9, 1981

Flower Stalls

Flower stalls on street corners broad parasols shield nature's
fragile jewels from the brazen sun
Flower stalls dot our town with fragrance, colour and joy
They catch my eye, my attention, my will
They pull me like the moon pulls the sea
Choosing is difficult
Which thing of beauty will I take with me?
The soft, the pale, the delicate?
The bright, the proud or the strong?
From the greenhouse or from the field?
Which thing of beauty will it be?
Which ones will turn their heads just for me?
Suzanne

May 31, 1981
Santa Barbara, CA

Le Bal

A clear half-moon
Shines her lopsided light
On a starry night
In another place, in another room
Rhythmic inviting dance music brings couples, friends, lovers
To step lightly, brightly to the melody
Crisp summer dresses, fluid party gowns move gracefully in the night air
A kaleidoscope - a succession of patterns and colours
I hear the festive sound
Animated voices and the laughter
The night has no beginning, it has no end
A mixture of lights, music and pretty dresses
All of it goes 'round and 'round
In another place, in another room
The music, the laughter, the whirling colours are remembered
A clear half-moon
Shines her lopsided light on me in another place, at another time, in another room

June 1981

Defiance

There were rules
Oh! there were rules
There were to be no flowers
None!
It made upkeep so very difficult!
And so, the lawn in its verdant sweep
Was never, ever punctuated by colour
There were no jonquils or tulips
Bobbing in the March wind
Or the April rain
No petunias, sweet peas or poppies to welcome Summer days.
She loved flowers.
She would leave soon
But, not before secretly planting tulip bulbs
On a gray November day
One hundred and fifty tulips went furtively
Into the dormant earth
They would not be seen until the following spring
Months after she was gone.
That was her act of defiance
In the face of unreasonableness

Suzanne Lafond
1981

Independence

INDEPENDENCE
What a ring it has to it!
Not subject to control by others
Not looking to others for one's opinions or for guidance in conduct
Not bound by, or committed to anything or anyone
Freedom to be:
Self-sufficient, self-contained, self-supported, self-sustained
Pillar of strength...
That is, Mondays through Saturdays
On Sundays, loneliness
Not due to mercurial instability
Or capricious changeability
Independents by nature don't wish to disturb, disrupt, impose or upset...
Their very sturdiness obscures the signals from the heart
Only those whose antennae are extended can detect the stifled sob
The muffled cry, the deep sadness that is sometimes within...

Suzanne   August 15, 1982

P. S. I was not aware, when I wrote this, that it was the 13th anniversary of Mamie's death in a car accident in which she was a passenger, in Ontario, August 15, 1969

Why Is It?

Why is it that great truths when turned into hackneyed phrases and popular sayings, make me tired?
Why is it that what our elders knew and repeated to us is dismissed as "Old Wives Tales" or outdated speeches?
Why is it that the new buzzwords or Modern Psychology cause my head to turn the other way?
The trite, the meaningless, the timeworn words of so many, well intentioned as they are, seem not to reach deeply enough and uplift not at all?
Is it because people like the sound of newfound knowledge?
Are the words "I understand" not esoteric enough?
A gentle look, the pressing of a hand, expressing warmth from the heart convey more than all the teachings we hear today.
It is good, nay, necessary to forget everything the mind has stored .
And respond to hurt, of whatever dimension, instinctively, in a truly visceral way.
It isn't how much we know, but that we apply what we know to our daily lives that matters
The proof after all is how we live...

Suzanne
September 1982

Something is Taken Away

It isn't any thicker than onion skin,
But it holds things safely together
The slices don't slip apart,
The oranges have their membrane
The heart, our tissues, the atmosphere
Like a handclasp, all are connected, contained, embraced
By a flexible, transparent film.
Trust is the gauze that envelops relationships
When the invisible bond is lost
Something irretrievable is taken away.

Suzanne Lafond
1982

Spring Shoes

When I was very young, on the street where I lived
There was a lady who wore green shoes, blue shoes and red shoes.
When it was winter, the snow covered the sidewalks and pedestrians seemed to move stealthily, their footsteps muffled by the snow.
Once the snow melted, the sidewalks bare once again, I heard the clickety click of heels pass my window.
I would run to the window to see for myself if I'd really heard what I thought I'd heard - that the snow was all gone? It seemed to happen overnight.
The lady down the street was on her way to work in the brightest green shoes I had ever seen.
Green was the color of hope, Mother often said. She was right of course,
Green is the color of Spring

Suzanne Lafond
December 1, 1983

June 14, 1995

Montréal/Montreal

Montréal, sais-tu a quel point je t'aime?
Ton histoire cicule dans mes veines
Ton Oratoire, rue Sherbrooke, Ste Catherine
Ta musique, tes peintres et leurs tableaux
Le va et vient des Montréalais, ton métro
Something about you constricts my heart
So many feelings of yesterday, of long ago
Tes chansons d'amour, l'histoire des colons
Ton courage, ton calme, tes époques turbulentes
My friends, my French and English friends
How we laughed, danced, sang and loved
Ton musée, l'opéra, ta symphonie, tes artistes
Vieux Montréal, Café André, Couvent du Sacré Coeur
All of us, all of it shaped and formed us, in this, the most beautiful city of North America
Cette ville recherchée de milliers de touristes
Pourquoi cette plaie, fermée depuis trois siècles est-elle ouverte à nouveau? There is so much anger now, such bitterness such hurt I bleed for you Montréal, I bleed for Québec, I bleed for Canada I bleed for the ten generations of Québecois who came before me - mes ancêtres, ces pionniers d'antan, ces colons qui ont cultivé la terre, qui ont travaillé à la sueur de leur front, qui ont chanté et dansé dans notre beau pays, la main dans la main entre voisins français, anglais, écossais, irlandais, syriens, grecs, arméniens Catholiques, Protestants, Juifs et Musulmans

Ils pleurent, their tears, their sobs, leurs sanglots
m'angoissent. Nos grands-pères, nos grands'mères, nos papas,
nos mamans,
Oncles et tantes, cousins et cousines
Pleurent dans le silence éternel
Montréal, Québec c'est le Canada!
Would you, could you abandon your child?
Orphelins, que ferions nous sans père et mère?
Canada, terre de nos aieux
Ton front est ceint de fleurons glorieux…

Suzanne Charlotte Lafond Le 9 janvier, 1996

Art class painting by Suzanne Lafond entitled "Mother and Child," under the supervision of art teacher, Gus Baker in Nashville, TN

Rwanda, One Man's Story

August 19, 1994

His name is Justin Gatebuke, his home is Kigali, Rwanda. Justin has been attending Meharry Medical College for the last two years. Justin has a wife. Her name is Clotilde, their three children, a son, Claude Bernard is 15, a daughter Beatrice is 14 and little Alice is 10. Clotilde and their three children are still in Africa. They have, in fact, been part of that hellish exodus from Rwanda to Goma, Zaire a few weeks ago.

Justin's family has seen first hand the massacres of hundreds of Rwandans. The horrors depicted on television, which we view from the comfort of our home, they know first hand. They have lost parents, friends and relatives. Clotilde herself has escaped death no less than three times. They know hunger and thirst. In a word, they know a hell I pray we will never know.

Their particular situation is further complicated by the fact that Clotilde is a Tutsi and Justin is Hutu. Justin's mother was a Tutsi, his father Hutu. Children in Rwanda take on the father's nationality. Justin and Clotilde's three children have physical characteristics of their Hutu grandfather. This has meant double danger for the family. In a desperate attempt to find food for the children, Clotilde decided to place the children in a Hutu refugee camp while she went to a Tutsi refugee camp. In a civil war-torn country, no one checks credentials to see who is on whose side. The killings are indiscriminate.

Justin was able to make contact with someone in Uganda. Not someone he knew personally, but only the name of a man. This Ugandan was asked to purchase airline tickets for Clotilde and the children with money Justin sent him. Tickets that would allow them to travel from Goma, Zaire to Uganda. It was a huge gamble. $500 is no small sum for Justin. Would the Ugandan run with the money, or would he do the honorable thing? The Ugandan was honorable. Clotilde and the children finally reached Uganda this week. They will get to Kampala, the capital, as soon as possible. There is an American embassy in Kampala and it is from this embassy that all final travel arrangements (documentation, visas etc.) will be made.

Justin has carried his indescribable grief alone, for some months now, powerless to come to the aid of his wife and children. A chance encounter after Sunday Mass at The Cathedral of the Incarnation, here in Nashville, a few months ago, gave me an opportunity to learn from him the details of his family's plight. No one should have to shoulder such a tragedy alone, surely. Thus began an effort mounted by several caring communicants at the Cathedral to help our new friend and fellow parishoner get his family to a safe haven in the United States. Mark O'Neil, Special Projects Director at Channel 4, has been a moving force behind Project Justin.

Justin's quiet demeanor belies his strength, determination and courage. He has a remarkable command of English in spite of the fact that he could not speak the language two years ago. He pleads his case in a straightforward way without belaboring the horrors he knows his family has endured or resorting to bloody descriptions of conditions in his country. He needs our help and soon.

The plan is to raise enough money to send airline tickets to Clotilde, Claude Bernard, Beatrice and Alice so they can begin their long voyage to Nashville. It will cost $1,700 for each of the tickets, a total of $6,800 for airfare alone. We would like to raise

$10,000 to allow for extras often incurred while traveling. What money is left over will be used to buy some of the necessities they have gone without for many months. Justin has recently completed his requirements for a Master of Science in Public Health at Meharry Medical College and he is now seeking employment in the field of Public Health.

The first leg of their journey to Nashville will begin at Entebbe in southern Uganda. You might remember the drama at Entebbe airport in 1976, where Israeli commando forces rescued the hostages held aboard an Air France plane by Palestinian hijackers. There is a nucleus of support (of all faiths) for the Gatebuke family which consists of only a handful of people, so far. We would like to see that circle expand in an ever widening way, like the pebble tossed in the pond, to reach all who have been moved by the plight of Rwandans.

There are always reasons for inaction, but at this critical time for the Gatebuke family, inaction could effect a terrible outcome.

Who among us has not cried out in frustration?: "How I wish I could help those poor desperate people." We want to help, but how? This is an opportunity for us to help and to see first hand how our support is used. We enjoy such abundance in this country; food, drink, goods in incalculable numbers, comfort, freedom .... on and on. Can we find it in our hearts to help a family begin a new life? Can we show them that our heart is in the right place? I already know the answer to that question, for I have heard from friends who want to be counted in with their contribution. I received a call from a total stranger two or three weeks ago. He and his wife had heard that we were making plans to aid a Rwandan family and they have pledged their support.

The Gatebuke Family in America

It has been nearly two years since Justin Gatebuke's family arrived in Nashville, from the African nation of Rwanda. Some of you will remember that Justin, who had been working on his masters degree in public health at Meharry Medical College, could not return to Rwanda to be with his family because of the civil war.

Through the generosity of The Tennessean readers, we were able to raise enough money for airfare to bring Justin's wife Clotilde, their son, Claude and their two daughters, Beatrice and Alice to join him in Nashville.

I often wonder how many of us could accomplish, in less than two years, what this family has been able to do. First of all, thanks to Metro schools and their program of English as a Second Language (ESL), the children learned to speak English well enough to eventually become assimilated in their respective classes. At the time, Justin's wife, Clotilde, while still very new to the city, bravely set out by bus to her own English speaking classes. She too, learned well and was able to pass Tennessee State exams to become a Nursing Assistant Technician. She is now employed at Trevecca in the Nursing Department. The two older children, Claude, now 18, and Beatrice, 16, are looking for summer jobs this year. Alice is 13 and will be at home this summer, she would welcome some baby sitting jobs.

I asked each member of the family what their biggest adjustment had been since arriving in Nashville. The very first thing they mentioned was the difficulty of not being able to communicate. The second adjustment was getting used to food "American Style."

Peach Cobbler Stories

Clotilde prepares the same meals at home they were accustomed to eating in Rwanda. Alice did say she had grown very fond of pizza. Alice says that in some ways she would like to go back in time to rejoin her friends left behind in Rwanda. She had a special friend, Claudine, whom she misses very much. Her sadness can be felt when she tells me that she does not know if Claudine is still alive or if she was killed during the civil war massacres.

The next big step for the Gatebukes has been to find a place to live which would allow them to spread out a little. All five have been living in a two bedroom, shoe-box-size apartment for two years. After an extensive search, they found a four bedroom house, with a nice yard, in a convenient residential neighborhood. I envy them the big magnolia tree, already full of blossoms, a few feet from their back door.

So many people who were aware of the Gatebukes's plight ask me how they are doing, from time to time. It is such a pleasure for me to speak of their accomplishments, their get-up-and-go, their work ethic, their perseverance, the ease with which they have adapted to a new culture, new foods, new language. In a word, to life in these United States. I am often moved at the sight of all five of them worshipping together at the Cathedral of the Incarnation on Sunday mornings. It seems only yesterday that we were hearing their accounts of the horrors of war in Rwanda. Claude, who appears to have grown a foot since he has been here, dispenses his duties as a server at Mass in a dignified and polished manner.

Because they own very little in the way of furnishings for their new home, it is possible that some of our readers have something the Gatebukes can use. Items such as end tables, lamps, desks and chairs, a couch or two, or bookcases. If you have such items, please call the Gatebuke residence in the mornings or after 5:00 PM, and let them know what you have and make arrangements which will be mutually accomodating to you and the Gatebukes. Knowing that the furniture you give the Gatebukes is needed, will be appreciated and cared for, should give you a great feeling. What is it they say about virtue being its own reward?

Many of us at the Cathedral of the Incarnation, who have known Justin and his family over the last few years, have great admiration for each of them in their individual and collective efforts to overcome the difficulties political refugees everywhere, must surely face, in establishing a life in new surroundings.

The Tennessean, 21 August 1998

Peach Cobbler Stories

Peach Cobbler Stories

1997 Granny Smith's Farewell Speech

April 19, 1998

In the words of a young TV news anchor, "Granny Smith Rocks!"

This happened to me after an interview in Cedar Rapids, Iowa. You know and I know he didn't mean in a rocking chair.

As I headed back to Nashville from Wenatchee last May, I thought about how the coming year was going to unfold for me. I understood that 8,000 grandmothers were interested in being the spokesperson for the Washington Apple Commission, therefore I had better put a lot into this job, so as to validate the Commission's choice.

I hope I did that.

Traveling around the country promoting the advantages of maintaining an active life, staying fit and having a healthy lifestyle has been a very rewarding experience. How we live determines how we age; but you already knew that!

There are many myths about growing old, who better than "Granny Smith" to explode them? I read recently something I thought was worth repeating: Time does teach us something. That age is not a loss, but an exchange: an exchange of wisdom for youth, grace for foolishness, love for lust.

Life is serious business, but I am afraid I would be missing a big slice of it if I did not look for and appreciate the humor along the way.

For example, I observed that:

Male TV anchors wear more make-up than I do!

Staff & crew at TV stations come out of the woodwork like ants at a picnic at the very mention of food!

That hotel mattresses are better on the side away from the telephone.

That no matter how many hotel rooms you occupy, radar guides you to the bathroom door in the dead of night, rather than out into the hallway.

That a rise in the road in Nebraska is considered a "hill."

That you learn a lot about somebody by the way they handle these three things: lost luggage, cancelled flights and rainy days.

Two of the most asked questions have been: "Do you get free apples for a lifetime?" "No, I buy them like everyone else".

"Is this like Miss America?"
To which I always answered: "Not hardly!"

I learned that everyone likes apples. With the exception of one crotchety old man in a supermarket who made darn sure I knew he didn't like apples at all.

You win some, you lose some.

You'll be happy to know that "Please" and "Thank you" still work wonders.

That "Senior Moments" happen! More times than I care to count, I would go blank on ingredients for any given recipe, even when it was MY own: "Was that 1/2 cup of sugar or 1/4 cup?" or worse yet, when I said: "I want everyone at Channel 2 to enjoy these apples from the Washington Apple Commission. The attractive TV anchor patted my arm, corrected me soto voce: "This is Channel 4." I remembered that I was at Channel 2 earlier that day or maybe the day before. Those of you in the audience who are in my age group know exactly what I mean!

One last observation: That 85% of life is showing up. Especially at 5:45 AM.

My dream team: Rita Brautigham, Kari Volyn and Steve Gibbs have been nothing short of wonderful, supportive and constant. Joanne Thomas at Total Travel is the Totally Organized Travel person. Joanne and my dream team made my travels run smoothly, without so much as a hiccup. Mother nature, on the other hand, caused flights to be cancelled, delayed or just plain bumpy.

As Granny Smith, I visited 53 cities and some 25 states. Jim Thomas was on to a good thing when he dreamed up the Granny Smith promotion. Grandmothers and apple pie! How beautiful is that?

Taxi Drivers were my road companions, everywhere. Every one of them had a story to tell. I heard about their wives, their pets, their hopes for their children, their dream of buying a house, even of difficulties in their marriage. One driver asked if he could give me a hug because his children so love their grandmother, the hug was to be from them. I was pleased to accept. Another "cabbie" informed me that he prayed. I told him that I prayed too. I asked if he were going to pray in a mosque, a church, a chapel or a temple?

He said no, I pray now. With that he pulled off the freeway, found a plot of grass, reached for his prayer rug in the front seat, faced East and began intoning his prayers to Allah! He was Muslim and it was sundown. I did wonder why he didn't pray before he picked up his fare, but who am I to get in the way of heavenly communication?

Well, I must not turn this into a sermon from the pulpit. I do want to take time, however, to tell the Apple Commission how grateful I am for the opportunity of being their 1997 Granny Smith. I will remember the experiences and the people I have met for a very, very long time.

Sixty years ago, when I left home for my first day of school, my mother advised me to work hard, have fun and make new friends. I took that to heart!

Merci, Maman!

The gala evening where ten finalists were announced and the winner presented. On the left was the prior year's winner, Marjorie Carlson.

Suzanne photographed the day after being selected as the 1997 Washington State Granny Smith

Peach Cobbler Stories

Now, here's a granny who embodies the polish of time

Frank Ritter

WHAT could be more American to the core than mom and apple pie?

Well, you might try apple pie and a grandma who defies the stereotypes about senior citizens. Maybe a Nashville granny who has traveled across the United States for a year promoting nutrition, exercise and senior issues. And, yes, also apples.

Ask Suzanne Lafond about it — if you can catch up with her. Soon she's celebrate her 67th birthday, she's mighty busy these days, even though her tenure as America's greatest granny ended a few days ago.

Plucked last May out of 8,000 grandmothers from all across the nation, she was named "Granny Smith" — "spokesgranny" for the apple growers of Washington state.

To compete to be the Washington Apple Commission's granny, one obviously has to be an actual grandmother. Lafond, the mother of three sons, already had three granddaughters at the time, and a daughter-in-law was pregnant with a fourth granddaughter, who is now six months old.

Granny Smith must also lead a healthy lifestyle. (Yoga and aerobics are favorites for Lafond). And she must be active in her community. (Lafond's list of associations with civic, charitable, church and business groups is long).

Granny Smith must be a senior citizen. Lafond was 65 when she was chosen, and in that regard, she remembers especially the parade at the Apple Blossom Festival in Wenatchee, Wash., the day before the "Granny Finale" that chooses Granny Smith, who is named for a brand of apple.

"The 20 grandmothers in the finals rode in antique cars in the parade," she recalls. "I was in a 1931 Ford convertible, and a young man beside the road yelled, 'Hey, Granny! You're older than the car!' I wasn't offended. I yelled back, 'No, I'm not! We're *twins!* The car and I were born the same year.'"

Lafond is not hesitant to give her age. She's proud to be 67 in a month, and it helps to look so apple-cheeked and blossomy.

"There are many myths about growing old," she explains. "Who better than 'Granny Smith' to explode them? I recently read something worth repeating: Time does teach us something. That age is not a loss, but an exchange — an exchange of wisdom for youth, grace for foolishness, love for lust."

During one year "Granny Smith" went to 53 cities and 25 states, Lafond preached that message. Meanwhile, back home in Nashville, she juggled her own business (she's an insurance specialist in long-term health care for the elderly); her modeling, radio work and TV commercials; church activity (lector and prayer group leader); and charitable and civic involvement.

Recently, she volunteered to raise funds for the non-profit Tennessee Foreign Language Institute here. And she used to be development director for WPLN. Nashville's public radio station.

Senior citizens are among her special causes. Too often, she says, seniors are ridiculed in general, and women in particular, by some. Thus, she declines to work in TV commercials that picture seniors as ditzy and inept.

"I really don't like the way older women are often portrayed in the media," Lafond says. "People can be active and healthy in their 60s, 70s and 80s. I know some remarkable people who are in their 90s, so there is really no age when we have to quit enjoying life."

For the last year especially, Lafond has enjoyed life on the road, criss-crossing the country as Granny Smith. The trek, she says, has taught her that you learn a lot about somebody by the way they handle three things: lost luggage, canceled flights, and rainy days.

She learned, too, that a sense of humor helps and relates this story to make the point:

"Taxi drivers were my road companions everywhere. Every one of them had a story to tell. I heard about their wives, their pets, their hopes for their children, their dream of buying a house, even of difficulties in their marriage.

"One driver asked if he could give me a hug because his children so love their grandmother, and the hug was to be from them. I was pleased to accept.

"Another cabbie informed me that he prayed. I told him that I pray, too. I asked if he were going to pray in a mosque, a church, a chapel, or a temple? He said 'No, I pray now.' With that, he pulled off the freeway, found a plot of grass, reached for his prayer rug in the front seat, faced east and began intoning his prayers to Allah! He was a Muslim — and it *was* sundown.

"I did wonder why he didn't pray before he picked up his fare, but who am I to get in the way of heavenly communication."

The message isn't new with Lafond, but she preaches it to those who will listen: "How we live determines how we age."

If you were to meet her, you'd agree that Lafond is aging pretty well. Like a good apple. ■

(Ritter is an editor and columnist for The Tennessean.)

Frank Ritter, an old friend, had kind words to write in The Tennessean newspaper about Granny Smith, 1997.

Peach Cobbler Stories

The twenty finalists in 1997 for the title of Granny Smith for the coming year. Suzanne is kneeling in the front row as the only one wearing sunglasses. How cool is that granny?

Suzanne, the new Granny Smith, sitting in her carriage. The vintage car was of the same vintage as that year's Granny Smith. It doesn't get any better than that!

"The Search for Granny Smith" promotion to find the 1997 Granny Smith to represent the Washington State Apple Commission for the year 1997-98. In the center of the photo is Suzanne Lafond, who was chosen among 8,000 applicants to represent the state of Washington. Wenatchee is the undisputed Apple Capital of the World! On her left is her very good friend, Marlene Pinck, who was also a guest of the Apple Commission to cheer on her longtime friend. Marlene and Suzanne have been friends since the age of 13, growing up very near each other in the suburbs of Montreal.

Suzanne, after being selected Granny Smith for 1997, a promotion for the Washington State Apple Commission

Peach Cobbler Stories

Publicity for Dress for Success – Nashville

A favorite quotation by Gertrude Stein that Suzanne included on this Dress for Success brochure: "A difference, to be a difference, must make a difference."

Dress for Success Moments 1998 – 2008

One afternoon, a young woman came to Dress for Success Nashville to receive a suit or separates. Basically an outfit appropriate to wear to a job interview. She came in by herself, joining three other women who were waiting their turn for me to "suit" them for their job interview.

It went very well and rather quickly as DFS had just the right sizes for each one. We were well stocked at that particular moment. I would bring suits in their size for their approval and the client would select the ones she wanted to try, or she could try as many as she wanted.

Fortunately, when DFS first rented space at Green Hills Court, I was able to turn one of the rooms into two fitting rooms, separated by canvas dividers on which the students from the O'More School of Design had painted broad stripes. That was a beautiful volunteer effort on the part of the O'More School. I had enough fabric to divide one room into two private dressing rooms.

That gave us the ability to see two clients at once. It made things more efficient for me, of course. There was always chatter and banter going on between each client and me, but I never invaded their privacy.

I gave them shoes, hosiery, handbags, scarves, cosmetics and whatever else the community would provide for the women we served. It was fun for them and more fun for me to see the excitement on their faces and in the physical way they strutted their stuff! They twirled in front of the mirror and even as they came out of the dressing rooms to show off their new suits to whomever sat in the waiting room, I think I was more excited than they were. Truly, they were transformed.

That day, after the three clients who had come together were outfitted and left with their suits, shoes, hosiery, jewelry, make-up etc., I turned my attention to the young woman who had come by herself.

Before I rushed out to begin locating suits in her size, I sat down with her to catch my breath, first of all, but also to visit with her a moment. There was something so beautiful about this young woman, I wanted to know more about her. Each client fills out a form with sizes: suit, blouse, shoes, etc., so she gave me the form. This was going to be her first job interview. I looked at the sizes she wore and told her, that because she was a size 8, I had many suits from which she could choose.

I have to explain that I had what was called a "Back Room" where the suits were kept and where the clients were not to enter. I'll explain why, later.

The young woman was shy and didn't share very much, so I proceeded to select some of the outfits in her size. She was very easy to fit, indeed. Everything she tried on looked beautiful on her. As she prepared to leave, gathering the suit and all the accessories, she put everything down and told me that she wanted to be like me. How she could present herself, comport herself, hold herself ... and could I teach her?

I was very touched by her remarks and my heart went out to her. I explained that I was operating DFS by myself and couldn't really afford the time to teach her outside this moment. I did say the following: "While you were watching me, I was watching you." She was a younger version of me. I told her that I observed how she spoke, how she handled herself and if she continued to be observant, she wouldn't need anyone to teach her. She could select from the people she looked-up to, the things she could easily assimilate into who she already was. I told her I thought she had good instincts. She smiled shyly. We hugged and I wished her all the good luck in the world. So many years later, I still think about this young woman and where she might be and the work she may be doing.

Another time, a young client came to be "suited" for her job interview. We were alone and again I sat with her a moment in the waiting room. Without preamble she asked me this question: "What does it mean when someone tells you, you're a nobody?" In turn I asked her if someone had called her that. She answered yes.

At the risk of sounding "preachy," I told her that God didn't have time to create a nobody. To call someone a nobody means that the person has no importance, or is of no influence. It is a very mean-spirited expression that is intended to demean someone. I explained that every one of God's creatures has value no matter where they came from, or what hardships they have known. I wanted her to repeat quietly to herself: "I have value and no one can take that away from me." To say it to herself especially when one goes through a rough patch on his/her journey. It will give one the confidence one needs. I promise, it will help you! Just remember: <u>You Do Have Value</u>!

I wanted to explain why the clients were not allowed into the "Back Room." When DFS opened its doors in the Fall of 1998, I approached Sister Sandra of Project Reflect to ask if she had a little room I could use to open DFS. At the time Sister Sandra was using Cockrill Elementary School for her great new Project Reflect, a nonprofit. Sister Sandra's work was dedicated to rescuing children who lived in the projects in Nashville. Often these children lived with a drug-addicted parent/parents and without question they needed rescuing. As a long-time educator, this became Sister Sandra's mission.

Project Reflect had the use of an abandoned Metro School building that had not been used for two or more years. Sister Sandra came to The Cathedral of the Incarnation (where I worship) and was introduced by Fr. Fleming. Sister Sandra had come to speak about her new school. She was looking for volunteers to help scrub and paint Cockrill Elementary School, so it would be clean and ready for her young charges.

I was one of a hundred plus volunteers and we soon got to work, scraping, washing, and some volunteers painted rooms. We pitched in to give the old school a real face-lift. I found myself on my knees or sitting on the floor scraping dried up stuff off the floor, old paint, oil and whatever else an old school building accumulates through the years. That is how I first met Sister Sandra, on my knees, scrubbing!

So, when I called her to see if she might have a small room to spare, she remembered me because I was probably the only white-haired person in the pack. Sister asked how much space I needed. I told her that a closet would do! She answered by asking if I could use a classroom? Really? What a gift that would be! We moved in after I spent time begging for used racks from stores around town. I did get help from Sister Sandra's "Go To" helper at Project Reflect. He became very important to me. With his truck, he picked up racks, chairs, a desk and other useful things I had simply found somewhere that could fit our needs at Dress for Success.

The racks we had were in the open classroom, round racks, long racks, shoe racks, lots of discard things by the community. Who knew we could build a nonprofit business with discarded items such as these?

The problem arose when I helped one client in this open classroom, the others gathered around the "unmanned" racks and got all the sizes out of place – never putting back anything according to size. The clothing I had taken great care in separating, were now in a mess. I had a couple of volunteers then and one of them told me that if we ever moved into a permanent space – Cockrill Elementary was our temporary home which I knew from the start - that for sure I should have a "Back Room," where clients were not invited to enter. Simply trying to keep order was an uppermost consideration. It was a helpful and positive comment to hear at that very moment. That is the "back story" behind the closed-off back room.

In order to soften the blow to the clients who would have preferred rummaging through the racks themselves, I explained time after time, that in the very best, most expensive boutiques, the sales people brought the garments to the clients and that is precisely what we were doing here at Dress for Success. Giving them a taste of the high life!

That did solve the problem except for one client who came with an advisor and an attitude. She asked if she could go into the back room and pick out what she wanted because she was in a hurry and I was helping two other clients and she couldn't wait. I reminded her that she was over 30 minutes late for her appointment and she must wait a few minutes. When I didn't grant her permission to go in the back room she said: "Lady you have a mouth on you!" As nicely as I could, I pointed out the obvious: There was only one of me, she arrived late while I was helping others and I couldn't drop everything to accommodate her. She was not happy. I think she tried to slam the door as she left…the door didn't slam! This may be a nonprofit, but rest assured, it does not guarantee that it will bring out the best in people.

Often the clients wrote thank you notes, sent a letter or a card. I kept these expressions of gratitude to DFS in a basket on the desk.

My method was to gently let them see that a 'Thank You' was always appreciated and an appropriate thing for them to do in life, generally.

One client wrote that her young son, seeing her in her suit as she was leaving for a job interview, said this to her: "Mama, I didn't know you could look like that!" That gave me chills and those are the things I choose to remember. Dress for Success Nashville was a very happy place in which to work. Hard work, but if I helped just one woman, I received blessings by the hundreds.

Dress for Success (DFS): Client examining her new suit

First open house for Dress for Success – Nashville at Cockrill Elementary School, thanks to Sister Sandra Smithson, who let DFS use rent-free one of the classrooms that Project Reflect did not need at the time. Shown: Suzanne Lafond and Cheryl Carpenter with a leading designer and strong supporter of DFS.

Dress for Success – Nashville: Suzanne Lafond welcomes the founder of Dress for Success – Worldwide, Nancy Lublin in April, 1999, for DFS's first open house in Nashville.

Mary Hance, known around town as Ms. Cheap because she seeks out bargains and good buys better than any sniffing police dog Suzanne ever knew, wrote this article on behalf of Dress for Success – Nashville. Suzanne attended a couple of events scheduled at the same time and place as Ms. Cheap. She talked about the work of finding savings in any and all areas for everybody, and Suzanne talked about the nonprofit DFS-Nashville. Ms. Cheap wrote about DFS – Nashville's needs in her column.. Ms. Cheap knows more about everything that goes on in Nashville, especially where those great bargains can be had!

Across the Clothesline October 2001

To feel great passion for what we do in life is to be fortunate indeed. To know such good fortune when we enter our **Third age** (those of us 60 and over) of life is to be twice blessed. Since launching Dress for Success Nashville in 1998/1999, next to family and friends, Dress for Success Nashville has occupied my heart, my energy and my time.

Seeing our clients leave our office, business suit in hand with a spring in their step, a smile and sometimes, a tear in their eye, makes the hard work pale by contrast. We are proud of having given a confidence boost to more than 600 women who are making the transition from welfare to work. Our numbers have grown every year, and DFS is working diligently to keep up with the demand.

We are looking to increasing our program by 30%. We will need your help in order to achieve our goal. Because 60% of our clients are a size 18 and larger, we have to purchase suits in that size range. Unfortunately for Dress for Success, those are not the sizes received from suit donors. We spend $65 for each suit and blouse we purchase for our full-figured clients.

Your financial support has become urgent. We feel deeply that we all benefit when the women who come to DFS Nashville succeed in finding jobs and in shaping better lives for themselves and their families. It is much more than a job…it is an opportunity for a new start on a career path and financial independence. Please help us continue this important and exciting work. You will help build a stronger community for all of us in the greater Nashville area.

Dress for Success Nashville has had steadfast friends from the time the idea was but a tiny seed to the reality of its presence in the community today. We will never forget our friends' generosity, their confidence in our ability to succeed and their sincere belief in the DFS mission. We are grateful for their ongoing support.

Our deepest thanks to so many of you who have understood the importance of helping disadvantaged women in our community. We are grateful for your financial assistance, your suit donations and your friendship. Keep in touch. We promise to do the same.

Suzanne Lafond
Executive Director
Dress for Success Nashville.

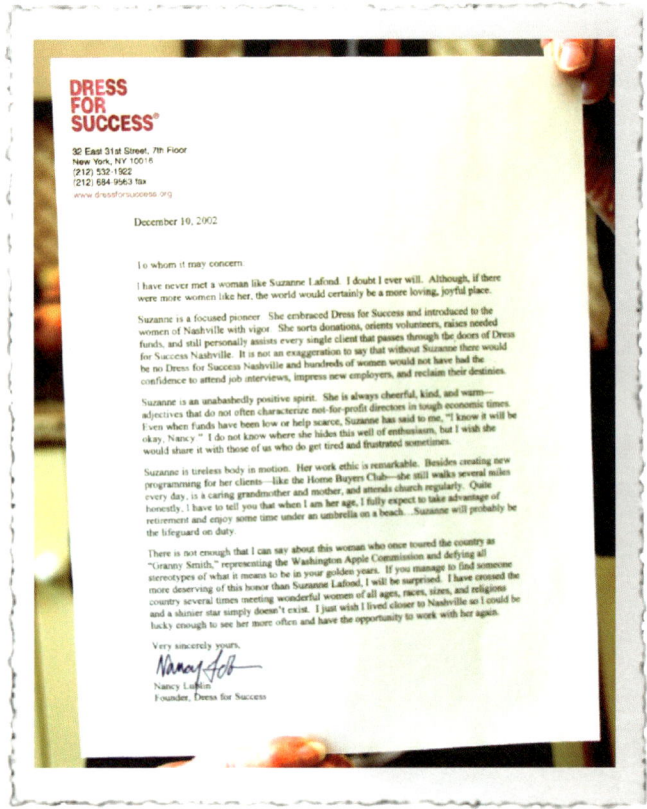

Here is a beautiful, generous and kind letter written about Suzanne and Dress for Success – Nashville by Nancy Lublin, the founder of Dress for Success – Worldwide. Nancy can now boast of having some 100 affiliates around the world. She is a gifted, intelligent woman who saw a need for women and tackled it head on. She was a great inspiration to Suzanne. Nancy's kind letter to Suzanne made her blush, but she will always be grateful to Nancy for allowing Suzanne to open an affiliate of Dress for Success in Nashville

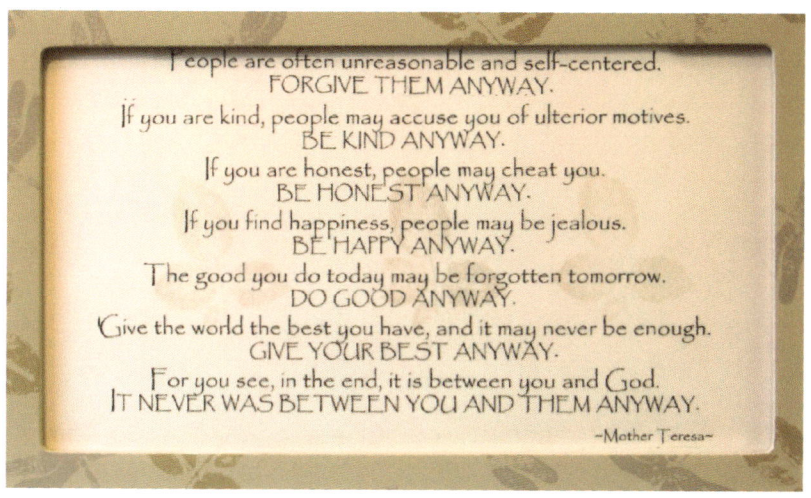

Mother Theresa's lasting words Suzanne had framed to hang in the office of Dress for Success – Nashville:
"People are often unreasonable and self-centered.
FORGIVE THEM ANYWAY.
If you are kind, people may accuse you of ulterior motives.
BE KIND ANYWAY.
If you are honest, people may cheat you.
BE HONEST ANYWAY.
If you find happiness, people may be jealous.
BE HAPPY ANYWAY.
The good you do today may be forgotten tomorrow.
DO GOOD ANYWAY.
Give the world the best you have, and it may never be enough.
GIVE YOUR BEST ANYWAY.
For you see, in the end, it is between you and God.

IT NEVER WAS BETWEEN YOU AND THEM ANYWAY."

-Mother Theresa

Suzanne among the flowers in Tennessee

Athena 2003 Awards

Question posed to the candidates: "When you leave this earth, what do you want to have caused, improved, changed or maintained as your life's legacy?"

A legacy is more accurately measured by successive generations. Ultimately, I leave it to those who follow to evaluate my efforts in all things.

My early Catholic education taught me that a spirit of sacrifice is an important rule of life. It also taught me that serving my fellow man, helping others along life's way was the most important aspect of my journey.

I have always enjoyed volunteering for all sorts of causes, even as a child. At school, at summer camp and later, at the age of 17, as a volunteer at the Canadian Red Cross. I was placed in the Motor Corps. I was to use a limousine with the Canadian Red Cross shield on the door to pick up six to eight blind persons and transport them to a recreation center once each week, and return them to their various residences. That was the assignment. A remark made by a blind young man, 18 years old, and one of my weekly riders, made a lasting impression on me. He said: "Some people have all the luck in this world." Insignificant as that now seems, it made me realize that I was one of those lucky people. Luck, over which I had nothing to do. An accident of birth, as I came to regard it. I trace back a desire to help others to those early years.

Sometime in 1994, I met a man at church from Rwanda, whose family, a wife and three young children, were still living there. It was at the time of the genocide in his country. A very bad time for the young family. There were problems with getting travel visas for the family and the cost was prohibitive in his circumstances. I was touched by his plight and I told him if he could work on getting the visas, I would raise the money for airfare for his family. In time, Justin got the visas and I was able to raise $10,000. Quite simply with a single letter written to the editor at the Tennessean. In a short time the entire family was reunited. I was very happy and grateful to the readers of *The Tennessean* and others who wanted to help the Gatebuke family.

I know that through my work at Dress for Success I have helped transform women into someone they didn't know they could become. Only 25% of what we do at Dress for Success is about suits. 75% of my efforts are spent in building up low self-esteem and a lack of self-confidence. Being dressed appropriately, whether we like it or not, makes a difference in how we feel and also in how we are perceived by others.

I think of the women who come through DSN as part of my extended family. If they act inappropriately, I am quick to let them know that a certain kind of behavior is not acceptable, just as I would react to my own children were they not acting appropriately. I realized early on that I cannot take for granted that the women we serve know what I know. We start with the basics. Whatever comes up is what we discuss. They are beautiful when they come through the door, although they don't know that. I remind them that they are. I assure them, as they leave, that I only changed their clothes. They have value, they have new knowledge and skills. They will make it in the workforce...and they do make it. They write me or call me to tell me they felt beautiful in their new suit. One of them wrote me that she felt "stand out gorgeous" and she "nailed the job."

I don't know what my legacy will be any more than I know what my destiny will be, but this I know: I find joy in helping others. Some years ago I came across this quotation attributed to Beaudelaire, and it stayed with me: "Et je me couche fier d'avoir vécu et souffert dans d'autres que moi même." Translated to mean... "And I lie down, proud to have understood someone else's pain."

My first thought regarding a legacy, concerns my three sons. The pride I feel in each one, their individual talents and accomplishments - that is my legacy. I observe each of my sons and their wives, now surrounded by beautiful daughters, and how, as parents, they are preparing their young daughters to be the women of tomorrow. That too, I will claim as my legacy.

Outside of family, I would like to have been instrumental in helping those who came to me at Dress for Success, to discover the self-confidence and self-worth they didn't know they had. At Dress for Success, we celebrate every woman's ability to succeed. Dignity and respect are the cornerstones of our service to each woman with whom we come in contact.

I would like to see the disadvantaged women I meet find independence. Independence, achieved by earning sufficient income to support themselves; by having the courage to leave an abusive situation. The resolve to show their children a better life outside public assistance; to seek treatment from substance abuse and as a result, to become free to do an honest day's work for an honest day's pay. Independence meaning, for example, the freedom to work for and buy a home. At Dress for Success we want to see our sisters realize their dream of homeownership. There is a kind of magic and ripple effect in being part of someone's dream.

There is so much we can do to foster better treatment of women in society: Can we not work toward affecting change in how women are portrayed in the media, for instance? Can we not make our views known with regard to television programs, publications or music, which insult the dignity of women or debase their role in society - that it is not acceptable to demean women? Women can and should prepare themselves for positions of responsibility and creativity in the media, not in conflict with masculine roles, but by impressing their own genius on their work and professional activity. That is a change I would like to see realized in my lifetime.

When I think of the original meaning of legacy, which is to entrust someone the duty or the right to do something – something handed down from a predecessor, I think of the pleasure I have had in teaching others what I know, entrusting them with the duty and the right to their own legacy. If I can do that, I might feel that my efforts have been fulfilled — then, God willing, my legacy will be the happiness and success of others.

More Peach Cobbler Stories

A recent PCS: I was meeting friends at Amerigo's, an Italian restaurant at 20th and West End. It is a noisy place on Friday nights with the patrons being easily fifty years my junior. It is summer and graduations are going on everywhere in town. After dinner, each one in my party headed out in a different direction.

I passed a group of young women lined up two deep outside the restaurant as if to have their picture taken. Another young woman from the group stood in the street ready to snap the photo. When I realized what they were doing, I back-walked a few steps, and still holding my "doggy bag," I took my stance dead center in front of the group and smiled. Snap, the photo was taken and all had a good laugh. Perhaps I am in the ether hovering somewhere among these young graduates.

Then there was a 5K for which I had signed up to benefit Girls on the Run - a nonprofit. On that Saturday morning dark, rain-soaked clouds were forecast for the day. The "start" gun fired and, as if it had punctured the darkest cloud, the rain began. A light rain at first, then torrents, I mean buckets of rain, for the entire time it took me to finish. I am not a speed demon, but a 78 year old woman determined to finish the race.

There were spotters scattered throughout the course also getting soaked. I spoke to each one and thanked them for the tough duty they had pulled that day. At least we were moving. A young fellow stood around the next bend. I asked "where is the finish line?" He pointed the way. I then asked "How am I doing?" and he answered "You are just a blur." We both had a good laugh. It helped us put up with the deluge because we looked like drowned rats.

My life is very ordinary as measured against people whose lives are extraordinary. I have no delusion about that. Lives of so many people I have admired such as Victor Hugo, Charles Baudelaire, Emily Dickinson, Mother Theresa, Holocaust Survivors, my sons: Marc, Christian and Eric Stengel, Chopin, Beethoven, Mozart and Bach. Plus all great musicians, outstanding dancers, gifted singers, oh, the list goes on, you know that. Please understand that is not the yardstick by which I measure myself. The list represents those I think to be extraordinary. I am in awe and amazed by those lives.

That said, this is my life, the only one I've had, have now and will have. I can tell you that it has been a very good life. I didn't say a perfect life, but a very, very good one. Full of happy and sad memories and my share of disappointments, like everyone's life from which I draw my Peach Cobbler Stories.

Just so you can know me better, I am an incurable romantic, a neat freak (don't squawk, I am not alone) and emotional. I cry when I hear children singing, beautiful music, poetry, happy and sad stories make me tear up. In a word, I could be thought of as being emotionally incontinent. I am not proud of that, to me it is an embarrassment and a curse. I don't see anyone else with that same condition. I don't know how to fix it. Glasses don't help, nor do migraine pills, exercise doesn't touch it, a glass of wine, well it can make it worse or totally reverse it, as I can be happy funny. Since I am coming out of the closet as this "cry-baby," I will let it all out: I have even cried at commercials that have touched me in a certain way. Who does that? Sometimes I think the connection to the tear ducts and the heart is simply an open valve with no "off" spigot. Life is too short and the problem too complex to try to figure it out, let alone fix it - probably the wiring system gone amuck. I will continue to live with it. Sorry, you'll have to live with it too.

Peach Cobbler Stories

Entering my senior years, (I call it my Dynamic Years) I have taken to participating in a few 5Ks. Let me specify, I am not a runner, but I "fast walk" and do a little jogging when I am still fresh! At first, I didn't pay much attention to the fact that people over 70 had a division called 70 to 100. In retrospect, I thought that was condescending, rude and unfair to seniors! Every other age division in these races has a 5 year increment. I took this on as my mission not only for myself, or for the current group of seniors, but (this was my battle cry), for the Baby Boomers who follow and WILL demand it!

Trophies: "Girls on the Run 5K" First place female in the 80-84 category, and Washington State Apple Commission finalist for the search for Granny Smith

Well, race organizers had a good laugh and would say: "Suzanne you win all the races in your division, the 70 to 100 year olds." I would say, never mind, I win because I am unopposed, but just you wait, the Boomers will come out in force 10, 20, 30 deep and the 80 year olds will not want to compete with a pup who is 70. Or a 70 year old woman would have her socks beaten off by a slip of a girl of 60. You follow? The good news is that most of the races in which I compete have changed the senior division to also reflect the 5 year increments. One battle won, YEAH!

While on the subject of 5Ks. When my youngest son, Eric, knows that I have entered a race he will ask: "How did you do Mom?" I puff myself up and declare that I won my division. Eric then looks at me with his penetrating dark eyes and says; "Did you have any competition?" I return the questioning gaze and say: "Eric, that is just plain rude. When you won a prize have I ever asked you if you had any competition?" We both laugh because I cannot tell a lie, I don't have any competition (so far) and it means that I win the race (only in my division of course) because it is called "showing up."

That is my mantra. Hollywood legend Marlene Dietrich long ago said: "95% of life is showing up." For the local 5Ks I entered, showing up is 100% of the race won in the 80 Plus division! I show up…

Headshot for "The Book," a must for print and runway

More photos in Suzanne's "Model's Book"

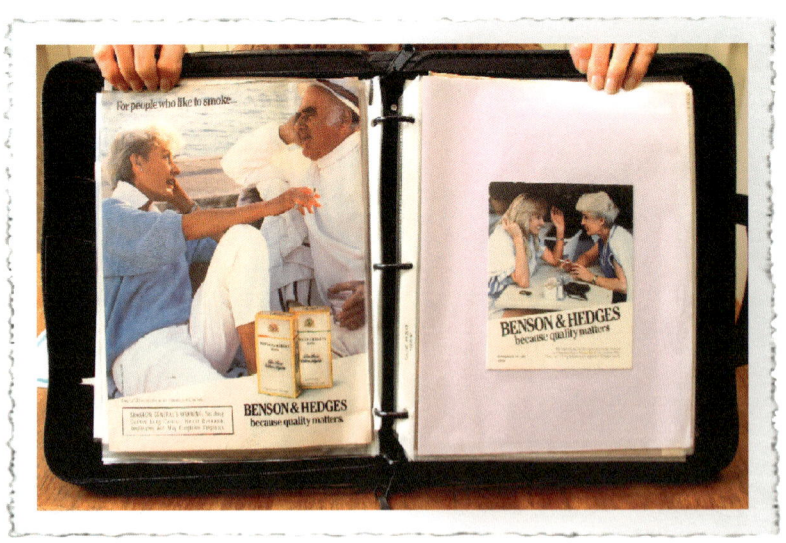

Advertising for Benson & Hedges in LA at the Marina

Photos from "The Book" carried to auditions in Los Angeles and Santa Barbara

Examples of Suzanne's print work

Print work for Richland Place brochure

Print work promoting a new specialty. At the time there were no law firms specializing in older clients. Suzanne was hired to appear in several print ads, brochures and television commercials aimed specifically at older people. That was a novelty then. Today there are Councils on Aging and a number of organizations geared primarily for Seniors. As the world observed that Seniors from different countries lived longer than their parents did, the creative entrepreneurs of the world began to target the white-haired army. Not a bad thing, just a shift in demographics.

Brochure for Baptist Hospital- Suzanne in shrimp-colored jog suit!

*Suzanne in ad for Green Hills Village & Mall, shown on the back cover of **Advantage**, The Nashville business magazine in July 1979. The ad copy reads: "Green Hills? Well, I remember when it opened back in '55. I've been shopping there ever since. Green Hills is the most convenient thing that ever happened to me." Mr. Sam Fleming is on the cover of the same issue. Mr. Fleming, former President and Chairman of Third National Bank, was a community leader for many years. He was known as a "mover and shaker" around Nashville.*

*Suzanne was featured and photographed in **Nautilus Magazine** in an article on working women.*

Peach Cobbler Stories

Headshot taken for talent agency work: Print, Runway and TV

Pleasant and Amusing Memories of a Two-Day Shoot March 11 & 12, 2013

This particular audition and call-back hinted at being something I would truly enjoy doing, IF I got the job!

I did get the job and joined quite a few other senior men and women at DR&A Studio on Willow St.

The first good omen was having my GPS guide me to the studio in less than 20 minutes. When I first got my GPS, about seven or eight years ago, for $25.00 at Wal-Mart, I instructed said GPS to always take me by "Pig Path." In other words, to avoid Freeways whenever possible. It doesn't take longer – it does, instead, take less time to one's destination because one avoids all the congested areas. I saw no other cars on my Pig Path. What I did see were neighborhoods and schools I had never seen. I like that.
No rush or push to change lanes at the right time, no nerves trying to find the exit ramp I needed. If you miss your exit, you find yourself 15 miles beyond your intended destination. I do a "jigue" when I arrive to the tune of: "I love my GPS, I love my GPS, I love my GPS…how did I ever get along without you?"

I arrived fresh and delighted to do the job at hand. I will not get into the waiting around one always has to put up with on all and any commercial shoot. That's just part of filming/taping.

The first day, all of us seniors had still photos taken with different facial emotions. Then there was a splendid lunch with choices for everyone's diet and appetite.

Soon it was time to go home around 3:30 or 4:00 PM.

The second day of shooting, my call time was 11:00 AM. That was wonderful as it allowed me a slower pace to repack my wardrobe and get myself as "camera-ready" as I could. We had wonderful help on that count when we arrived at the studio. Men and women had the pleasure of having several hair and makeup stylists at the disposal of this large group of seniors. Prepping took up the rest of the morning. My time before the camera was scheduled right after lunch. I hurried through lunch so that I would have time to brush my teeth – that's important to me!

I was told where to sit, to look into the camera and say my lines. "What! I asked?" I had not been given a script and furthermore, I was told the script had been changed from the audition script. Well, I will need a Teleprompter, I said. A Teleprompter was soon brought to the camera where I was and one of the crew began to roll it at the pace I needed to deliver the lines.

Camera began rolling…I began reading…director said cut! "Suzanne has a tear in her left eye"…makeup person came with tissue and powder in hand. I said to the crew: "You'll have to excuse me, I have a problem with teary eyes…it is called "Emotional Incontinence." Well the crew laughed far too long, but I was enjoying the reaction. Then it was decided that this 5 foot tall senior needed a booster under her chair. I'm used to this, I have to stand on a box or sit on a booster for most commercials. The boxes are called apple boxes and come in varying heights. The crew assembled 2 boxes end-to-end and placed the chair on top of them. As I sat down I broke the chair. I said, I am so sorry, I should have known that my 250 lbs. frame could break this chair. For those who don't know me, I weigh 112 lbs. The crew and the director had a hearty guffaw.

Now in the new chair, we are set to return to the taping. One airplane flew overhead. We stopped until the sky was clear of air-traffic. The director signaled to go back to the beginning. I began and midway through my lines, I heard the hum of another airplane approaching. I kept reading, but I was pointing to the sky and said "I want to be on that plane to Santa Barbara!" Of course we had to stop, yet again, because of traffic in the sky. More laughter from the crew.

Before returning to the script, the director said: "Have you been a comedian in your lifetime?" To which I responded: "No, I'm Canadian!" More laughter from the room. I found this quite intoxicating!

However, the show must go on. I began reading my part once more, this time without interruption. The director liked it, the Buntin Agency liked it and the Director said "It's a wrap!" With that, I jumped up from my chair and everyone in the room applauded.

When I stepped down from my platform, Jeffrey Buntin, the grandson of this well known advertising agency came to me, hugged me, and said "You were wonderful!" He asked one of the photographers to take a picture of both of us and soon thereafter, I left the set. Being a part of the Brookdale commercial shoot doesn't get any better than that! This I know…The Crew, the Director, the Buntin Agency folks, the Hair & Makeup Department, the DR&A Studio personnel, the Craft people with their excellent food, other seniors on this shoot, made for time well spent with a great deal of appreciation on my part.

This is not a product endorsement, nor am I signaling any one in particular. It was a cohesive, thoughtful effort on everyone's part and I am happy to have been included.

A Prayer As We Grow Older

Lord, thou knowest better than I know myself, that I am growing older and will someday be old. Keep me from the fatal habit of thinking that I must say something on every subject and on every occasion. Release me from craving to straighten out everybody's affairs. Make me thoughtful but not moody: helpful, but not bossy.

With my vast store of wisdom it seems a pity not to use it all; but Thou knowest Lord, that I want a few friends at the end.

Keep my mind free from the recital of endless details; give me wings to get to the point. Seal my lips on my aches and pains; they are increasing, and love of rehearing them is becoming sweeter as the years go by. I dare not ask for grace enough to enjoy the tales of others' pains, but help me to endure them with patience.

I dare not ask for improved memory, but for a growing humility, and a lessening cocksureness when my memory seems to clash with the memory of others. Teach me the glorious lesson that occasionally I may be mistaken.

Keep me reasonably sweet; I do not want to be a saint…some of them are so hard to live with…a sour person is the crowning work of the devil. Give me ability to see good things in unexpected places and talent in unexpected people, and give me, O Lord, the grace to tell them so. AMEN

Found this somewhere and wanted to carry it with me as the years roll by! Author unknown.

The Cycles of Civilizations

An article I read in *The Tennessean* said the world's great civilizations averaged a cycle of 200 years. Those societies progressed through this sequence:

From bondage to spiritual faith.
From spiritual faith to great courage.
From great courage to liberty.
From liberty to abundance
From abundance to selfishness.
From selfishness to complacency.
From complacency to apathy.
From apathy to dependency.
From dependency back again into bondage.

Since the United States has passed its 200th anniversary, in view of the recent epidemic of immorality, what is America's current position in this cycle?

Biography

Suzanne Lafond was born, raised and educated in Montreal, Canada. She is a tenth generation French Canadian. All of Suzanne's schooling took place in Montreal. She studied fine art at l'Ecole des Beaux Arts de Montreal with business courses at Sir George Williams College, Montreal.

In 1982, she worked for the Bank of Montecito in Santa Barbara. Suzanne's work was "outside the Bank," seeking and recruiting commercial accounts for the Bank of Montecito. Suzanne came up with the idea of having a security pick-up for businesses on Stearn's Wharf. Business owners did not park on the Wharf as there were limited spaces reserved for tourists and customers. It was offered as protection, in the evening when business owners walked to their cars with the day's receipts in briefcases. An attack on a business owner had come to her attention and the seed of a security pick-up at the end of the business day was born. The bank officers felt this was a good idea for the business owner and the bank acquired new commercial accounts in this way.

For a brief period, she worked at Santa Barbara Winery as a wine representative in Santa Barbara and Los Angeles. She was trained by winemaker, Bruce McGuire, and she had Pierre Lafond as a go-to person for additional information with all questions.

In 1983, Julia Child called to ask if Suzanne might be interested in applying for a job as "West Coast Publicist" for the taping of *Dinner at Julia's*. The new 13 week series taped for WGBH in Boston. The taping took place in Santa Barbara. After a couple of interviews with Bob, Julia's attorney from Boston, Julia and Paul, she was asked to join the team at the home of Fess Parker, where the kitchen had been reworked to accommodate the television camera. That became the studio for the entire series.

After the work on *Dinner at Julia's,* Suzanne enrolled at the Los Angeles Broadcasting School (LAB). She was pursuing radio work at that time. After nearly two years in Los Angeles, Suzanne returned to Santa Barbara and was hired as a radio announcer at KKSB, a Jazz and Big Band format. She was on-air three days each week and the rest of the time she was actively selling airtime for the station. She also wrote, voiced and produced commercials for the new accounts she signed on for the station. It was good to put in practice what she had learned at broadcasting school. Many hours were spent at KKSB.

Suzanne returned to Nashville, Tennessee in 1988. She purchased condo #226 at Arden Place on Belmont Park Terrace in Nashville. It might interest you to know that she sold her condo in Santa Barbara, CA in one day! The buyer paid cash for double the amount Suzanne had paid for the condo. At the time, Suzanne purchased a condo in Santa Barbara on North Salsipuedes, which had been repossessed by the bank. Since the bank was not in the real estate business, they were glad to find a buyer – that was in 1982 – a good time for me to buy property.

Suzanne has been a resident of Nashville since 1956. She was a co-founder (with Cheryl Carpenter) and Executive Director of Dress for Success Nashville, an affiliate of Dress for Success Worldwide. The seed of Dress for Success Nashville began in the Fall of 1997, when my year as Granny Smith for the Washington State Apple Commission ended.

Professionally,

- French teacher at Ensworth School around 1966

- Development Director at WPLN - Public Radio 1976

- Recruiting and training interpreters for the 1983 Pre-Olympic trials in Santa Barbara.

Los Angeles Olympic Organizing Committee (LAOOC) in 1984. Director of Language Services at Lake Casitas venue, for the Olympic Regatta: Rowing, Canoeing, Kayaking.

Independent Insurance Broker, specializing in Long Term Care Insurance (LTC). 1991 – 2001.

- 1997-1998 Spokesperson for the Washington State Apple Commission with the title of Granny Smith. Suzanne visited 53 cities speaking to grandparents about staying fit, having a healthy lifestyle and encouraging everyone to be active in their communities. Suzanne is always proud to note that she was selected among 8,000 participants!

- She also does a fair amount of television commercials and radio spots as well as some print work

- In 2003, Suzanne was one of 26 nominees for the ATHENA award, in recognition of her contribution to the welfare of the community in Nashville, TN.

- Suzanne attends The Cathedral of the Incarnation on West End, where she is a Lector as well as the lector coordinator for the weekend Masses.

- She has three grown sons, three wonderful daughters-in-law, seven beautiful granddaughters and several grand-dogs.

LETTERS

MANGLING FRENCH

That's it! I have held my tongue long enough. Since 1954, in fact. I can no longer contain myself. I really thought Nashville would self-correct. It hasn't.

If Nashvillians are so intent on using French words or phrases in naming their establishments, their menus or their events, *Mon Dieu*! Why do they not ask someone who speaks and writes French (correctly) to help them achieve the desired effect?

Je suis très ennuyée (fed up!) of reading such things as "Un Eté du Vin" [sic], "Jeudi Fête" [sic] and other misuses and misspellings on a wide variety of programs, announcements, menus, etc., *j'en perds la tête* (going bonkers).

Nashville is not a sleepy town down South and should not project a country bumpkin image any more than necessary to our international cousins et cousines. Continuing this trend does a fine job promoting just that.

Remember, this is the Athens of the South. There are French departments at every turn and francophones on every corner.

Check it out, *s'il vous plaît*. And, it wouldn't hurt one bit to learn to pronounce it either. Mère Bulles (which is a sorry choice for what Rodney Wise wanted to say), is not Mère "Bull." Not here, not in France, not in French Canada, not in Algeria, not in Cameroon.

Parlons le français souvent et parlons-le bien! (Let us speak French often and let us speak it well.)

Suzanne Lafond
4400 Belmont Park Terr., #226, Nashville

Peach Cobbler Stories

Hand-Writing Analysis

11/28/86

SUZANNE LAFOND

371 BARHAM BLVD 5-203 LOS ANGELES, CA 9036

DEAR READER:

THANK YOU FOR RESPONDING TO THE HANDWRITING ANALYSIS OFFER IN PARADE MAGAZINE. THIS COMPUTER—PRINTED ANALYSIS OF YOUR HANDWRITING HAS BEEN PREPARED BY A TEAM TRAINED AND SUPERVISED BY GRAPHOLOGIST CARLOS PEDREGAL.

HERE IS THE RESULT Of YOUR ANALYSIS, WHICH IS CONFIDENTIAL, OF .COURSE. THE FOLLOWING PARAGRAPHS DESCRIBE THE DOMINANT CHARACTERISTICS OF YOUR PERSONALITY AS REFLECTED BY YOUR HANDWRITING.

GOOD TASTE:

YOUR HANDWRITING REVEALS THAT YOU ARE A PERSON OF TASTE. THIS RATHER SPECIAL CHARACTERISTIC IS VERY IMPORTANT, FOR IT HAS A TWOFOLD INFLUENCE ON YOU AS REGARDS CHOICE

AND DIRECTION IN LIFE. WHEN CHOICE COMES INTO PLAY, YOUR GOOD TASTE WILL PREVENT YOU FROM CHOOSING JOBS AND FROM ASSOCIATING OR LIVING WITH PEOPLE OF WHOM YOU CANNOT APPROVE. AS FOR DIRECTION, ITS INFLUENCE WILL INEVITABLY DRAW YOU INTO UNDERTAKINGS THAT WILL ENABLE YOU TO DEVELOP FULLY YOUR ARTISTIC CAPACITIES AND AESTHETIC SENSE.

IF YOU CAN MAINTAIN A RELATIVE EQUILIBRIUM, IN A FAVORABLE SETTING PROPITIOUS FOR YOUR PERSONALITY, YOU WILL BE VERY HAPPY AND FEEL FULFILLED.

EMOTIONAL SKEPTICISM:

YOU HAVE BEEN DEEPLY HURT, AND THE CONSEQUENCE HAS BEEN AN EXTREMELY STRONG EMOTIONAL SKEPTICISM.

THE SUBSEQUENT DECISION YOU MADE ABOUT ROMANCE WAS DESIGNED TO PREVENT YOU FROM EASILY GIVING YOUR HEART ONCE AGAIN. YOUR ATTITUDE IS TIMOROUS OR, WORSE STILL, INDIFFERENT.

YOU HAVE SUFFERED A GREAT DEAL, BUT THAT IS NOT SUFFICIENT REASON TO ELIMINATE LOVE FROM YOUR LIFE. TENDENCY TO BE TYRANNICAL

THERE ARE DEFINITE TENDENCIES TOWARD BOSSINESS IN YOUR HANDWRITING. IT IS DIFFICULT TO DETERMINE THEIR ORIGIN, BUT THEY PROBABLY ARISE FROM PROBLEMS OF AN EMOTIONAL NATURE. ON THE SEXUAL LEVEL, YOU ARE ALWAYS ON THE DEFENSIVE.

THIS INHIBITION MAY HAVE CONDITIONED YOUR CHARACTER AND MADE YOU TYRANNICAL IN OTHER FIELDS AS A SORT OF REVENGE FOR YOUR EMOTIONAL DEFICIENCIES.

IT IS IN YOUR INTEREST TO FACE UP TO YOUR PERSONAL PROBLEMS OBJECTIVELY: THE CHANGE WILL COME ABOUT NATURALLY.

ALTRUISM:

YOUR COMPLETE REGARD AND CONSIDERATION OF OTHERS BEFORE YOURSELF CAN INVOLVE YOU IN DIFFICULT SITUATIONS. YOU REALIZE IT, BUT STILL CONTINUE TO DISPLAY YOUR GENEROSITY. YOUR PERSEVERING UNSELFISHNESS IS ADMIRABLE IN OUR EGOISTIC TIMES.

WE CANNOT ADVISE YOU TO CHANGE YOUR WAYS, EVEN THOUGH MANY OF YOUR ACTIONS WILL NOT BRING YOU THE GRATITUDE YOU DESERVE, SO CONTINUE TO ACT ACCORDING TO YOUR CONVICTIONS.

AMBITION:

YOU DISLIKE HALF MEASURES. PERSONAL EFFORT AND DETERMINATION ENABLE YOU TO ATTAIN THE GOALS YOU HAVE SET FOR YOURSELF. NEVERTHELESS, YOUR AMBITIOUS CHARACTER IMPOSES GOALS THAT BECOME MORE AND MORE DIFFICULT TO ATTAIN. BY CONTROLLING YOUR IMPETUOSITY AND AMBITION, YOU WILL ACHIEVE BETTER RESULTS.

WORK CAPACITY:

DECISION, ENERGY AND A CAPACITY FOR WORK ARE UNMISTAKABLE CHARACTERISTICS OF YOUR PERSONALITY.

YOU ARE AN ACTIVE AND EFFICIENT PERSON, CAPABLE OF ATTAINING THE GOALS YOU SET FOR YOURSELF.

THE ABOVE ARE THE FUNDAMENTAL CHARACTERISTICS OF YOUR PERSONALITY ACCORDING TO YOUR HANDWRITING. AN ANALYSIS OF THE COMBINATION OF THESE CHARACTERISTICS WAS CARRIED OUT IN ORDER TO DETERMINE THE PRESENCE OF SPECIFIC TENDENCIES OF BEHAVIOR. IN YOUR CASE IT DID NOT REVEAL ANY PARTICULARLY EXAGGERATED TENDENCY.

I HOPE YOU HAVE FOUND THIS ANALYSIS INTERESTING AND THAT IT WILL BE PROFITABLE TO YOU.

WE ARE ALL AWARE OF HOW DIFFICULT IT IS TO GET TO KNOW OURSELVES.

BEFORE YOU MAKE A DEFINITIVE JUDGMENT ON THE RESULTS OF THIS ANALYSIS, LET YOUR FAMILY OR CLOSE FRIENDS READ IT. THE OPINION WE HAVE OF OURSELVES FREQUENTLY DOES NOT CORRESPOND TO THE REALITY. WE ARE GENERALLY EITHER TOO SELF-INDULGENT OR TOO CRITICAL OF OURSELVES. AND VERY OFTEN, EVEN CLEAR CONTRADICTIONS ARE INHERENT IN US.

THANKING YOU FOR YOUR CONFIDENCE, I AM,

SINCERELY YOURS, CARLOS PEDREGAL

*Suzanne, with her completed memoirs,
June, 2013*

In Closing...

I have collected, as best I could, bits and pieces of my life.

This introspection brought forth thoughts and feelings set aside long ago. Overall, the nine month project was positive, if somewhat daunting. How does one compress 82 years of life without going overboard?

Well here they are: MY PEACH COBBLER STORIES!

Unbeknown to Eric, who never thought that his teasing about my stories would end up as the title to my "memoirs!"

I hope my granddaughters will not be bored to death, but perhaps, in the end, they will know me better.

Allow me to share a serious thought in a reading that has been meaningful in my life.

A Tug on the Kite String

There is a story I once heard which seems to describe "religious experience" very well. It is a story of a small boy, flying a kite. The kite is surrounded and hidden by a low-flying cloud. A man comes along and says to the boy, "Hey kid, what are you doing with that string in your hand?" The boy replies, "I'm flying my kite." The man looks up and says, "I don't see a kite up there." The boy responds, "I don't either, but I know that there is a kite up there. I feel tugs on the kite string."

"Quiet Moments" with John Powell, S.J., a Jesuit Priest.

My Seven Beautiful and Intelligent Stengel Granddaughters

Mary Elizabeth, Morgan Elen, Sara Sudekum

Zoelie Ineza, Kaia Muhiza

August Knauer and Marie Sudekum

Be Brave
Be strong
Be flexible
Be adventurous
Be wise
Believe in yourself

Know that It Can be Done even while others think it cannot.

Be thoughtful toward others.

Be prayerful – remember prayer can be as simple as a conversation with God.

Above ALL, know that you are loved.

Mamie or Grandmère - Suzanne Charlotte Lafond Stengel

June 20, 2013

CPSIA information can be obtained
at www.ICGtesting.com
Printed in the USA
LVIC06n0245270713
344527LV00001B